Epic Fiction

Epic Fiction
The Art of Rudy Wiebe

W.J. Keith

The University of Alberta Press

First published by
The University of Alberta Press
Edmonton, Alberta, Canada
1981

ISBN 0-88864-075-7

copyright © The University of Alberta Press 1981

Canadian Cataloguing in Publication Data

Keith, W.J. (William John), 1934-
    Epic fiction

    ISBN 0-88864-075-7

    1. Wiebe, Rudy, 1934-   — Criticism and
    interpretation. I. Title.
    PS8545.I39Z74   C813'.54   C81-091229-5
    PR9199.3.W53Z74

Printed by
Hignell Printing Limited
Winnipeg, Manitoba

"If you don't know where you are and where you come from you're more or less like an animal that has no memory."

Rudy Wiebe in an interview with Eli Mandel, 1974

Contents

Preface

Rudy Wiebe is fast establishing himself as one of the most gifted and ambitious of Canadian novelists. He is also one of the more difficult, at least at a first encounter, and this book is intended as a general introduction that will, I hope, assist the reader's entry into an absorbing fictional world and so increase his enjoyment of Wiebe's work as a whole. I have included details of the writer's life and background when these seemed relevant to a full appreciation of his novels and short stories, but the subtitle, "The Art of Rudy Wiebe," indicates my central concern. Although he is decidedly in mid-career, he has already produced a body of work that cannot be exhausted in any single study (one could write a whole book about *The Scorched-Wood People* alone). Perhaps the most noticeable feature of his achievement as a novelist is the fact that, whereas his themes and preoccupations remain relatively stable, his approach to them, and particularly his artistic treatment of them, develop and mature. In the chapters devoted to individual novels I have therefore tried to assist the interested reader in coming to terms with Wiebe's ever-increasing artistic complexity.

Peace Shall Destroy Many and *First and Vital Candle,* for all their distinctive qualities, are relatively straightforward novels. One can, as it were, walk round them and recognize their clear shape. The novels from *The Blue Mountains of China* onwards, however, are encompassing; their "epic" features present the reader with a considerable artistic challenge. In discussing these novels I have deliberately concentrated on the literary problems that need to be clarified before any informed critical appreciation becomes possible. Most often these are concerned with structure and, in the case of the historical novels, with genre. Since Wiebe's thematic continuities guarantee a palpable though not always smooth development from one novel to another, my aim has been to establish the unique artistic qualities of each work.

In the course of writing this book, I have been substantially assisted by two colleagues. R.P. Bilan read and criticized an early draft, and (whatever its deficiencies may be) the final version has benefited from his firm scrutiny. Magdalene Redekop was also extremely helpful in providing information about the Mennonite background to Wiebe's work and offering stimulating suggestions about the Mennonite novels. My thanks are also due to Norma Gutteridge, director of the University of Alberta Press, for her advice and encouragement while the final version was being prepared, to Robert and Jean Tener for generous hospitality while I was examining the Wiebe papers in the University of Calgary, and to the Humanities and Social Sciences Committee of the University of Toronto Research Board for a travel grant that enabled me to visit Alberta while the book was in progress. I am also aware of the debt I owe to a number of librarians, and to various employees of McClelland and Stewart, for their helpful and cheerful assistance during my initial research.

Extracts from Rudy Wiebe's novels and short stories are quoted by kind permission of the Canadian publishers, McClelland and Stewart, Limited, Toronto.

I have incorporated into the text a number of sentences that first appeared in my introduction to the New Canadian Library reprint of *The Blue Mountains of China* (McClelland and Stewart, 1975) and in a review of *The Scorched-Wood People* published in the *Canadian Forum* (December 1977-January 1978). Otherwise, the material here offered appears for the first time.

W.J. Keith,
University College,
University of Toronto

June 1981

Abbreviations and References

In chapters devoted to individual novels, page-references without abbreviations refer to the novel being discussed. Otherwise the following abbreviations are employed for full-length works. (Where both hardcover and paperback editions exist, pagination is identical.)

AC   *Alberta/A Celebration* (with Tom Radford and Harry Savage). Edmonton: Hurtig, 1979.

BMC   *The Blue Mountains of China*. Toronto: McClelland and Stewart, 1970. (New Canadian Library, 1975)

FES   *Far As the Eye Can See* (written in collaboration with Theatre Passe Muraille). Edmonton: NeWest Press, 1977.

FVC   *First and Vital Candle*. Toronto: McClelland and Stewart, 1966.

PDM   *Peace Shall Destroy Many*. Toronto: McClelland and Stewart, 1962. (New Canadian Library, 1972)

SWP   *The Scorched-Wood People*. Toronto: McClelland and Stewart, 1977. (New Canadian Library, 1981)

TBB   *The Temptations of Big Bear*. Toronto: McClelland and Stewart, 1973. (New Canadian Library, 1976)

VL   *A Voice in the Land: Essays By and About Rudy Wiebe*. Edited by W.J. Keith. Edmonton: NeWest Press, 1981.

WV   *Where is the Voice Coming From?* Toronto: McClelland and Stewart, 1974.

1 Introduction

In his first novel, *Peace Shall Destroy Many*, Rudy Wiebe presents an incident which, when we return to it after reading his later and maturer work, reveals itself as central to his overall fictional vision. Thom Wiens, a young Mennonite in northern Saskatchewan, stumbles while preparing for hay-mowing and discovers a buffalo skull embedded in the earth. It is a moment of revelation:

> Staring at the broken skull, its heft heavy in his hands, a vista opened for Thom. Why was Canada called a "young" country? White men reckoned places young or old as they had had time to re-mould them to their own satisfaction. As often, to ruin. The memory of the half-Indian woman he had met last winter . . . forced itself upon him. . . . The aura of impenetrable consciousness of her own being that she carried like a garment somehow enveloped him, now as then. . . . Still holding the skull, he welcomed the thought of Two Poles at the picnic. Perhaps some lone ancestor of his had lain all day under the willows with the insects and bugs, spear or gun in hand, waiting for this buffalo to graze closer. (*PDM*, 82-3)

Thom's parents, like Wiebe's, came to Canada from Russia in 1930. As Mennonites they brought with them what Thom calls a few moments later "the traditions of the fathers" (*PDM*, 86), and began to carve out a new life in a supposedly new country. What Thom realizes as he looks at the buffalo skull is the lack of connection between the history of his own people and the history of the land upon which they live.[1]

This is, of course, a representative North American experience, but its resonances affect Wiebe with particular force. Born in a one-room log cabin in Saskatchewan in 1934 "in what would become, when my father and older brother chopped down enough trees for the house, our chicken barn,"[2] he is none the less a Canadian at two removes from the Canadian land, separated not only by the traditions and beliefs of his people but also by their language (he did not begin to speak English until he went to school). Again, given the diversity of Canada's immigrant population, this is—or, at least, was—not unusual, especially on the prairies where the original settlers included Ukrainians, Scandinavians, Icelanders, etc., as well as Mennonites. Wiebe has himself emphasized the fact that the Canadian west is "more mixed racially than any other part of Canada."[3] But he grew up at a time when the cultural heritage of those who belonged neither to the English- nor to the French-Canadian peoples was just beginning to make its mark on imaginative writing. It was also a time when the history of the native peoples was arousing interest as a new generation began to scrutinize its national inheritance.

In *Wolf Willow* (1955), a book praised by Wiebe in an early article,[4] Wallace Stegner wrote about his discovery later in life of the history of the prairie in which he had spent his childhood, a history no one had explained to him at the time. "There was the stuff of epic there," he wrote, "and still is for anyone who knows it right—perhaps for some *métis* or Cree, a descendant of Gabriel Dumont or Big Bear or Wandering Spirit, who can see the last years of the Plains frontier with the distance of history and with the passion of personal loss and defeat."[5] This sentence reads now as a remarkable anticipation of the author of *The Temptations of Big Bear* and *The Scorched-Wood People,* where the epic mode combines with fictional form and historical reconstruction. That the writer who accepted Stegner's proffered mantle should be a

Mennonite rather than a Métis or Indian should not surprise us. From his own people Wiebe inherited a religious vision, a seriousness of purpose, and a painful experience as a minority ethnic group living close to the land. Through creative understanding, he has become a spiritual descendant of Dumont, Big Bear, and Wandering Spirit; he has made the history of Western Canada his own.

Wiebe has emphasized again and again the richness of the Canadian historical past so often unrecognized because it is a past of the land but not of those who now inhabit the land. He sees his own family experience in northern Saskatchewan as representative. "One always had a sense," he told Eli Mandel, "that we were the first who came here, and that before we were here, that is before 1932, there wasn't anything here" (*VL*, 151). His own realization of this paradox recalls Stegner's. "It wasn't until years later," he remarks, "I discovered that the three miles my sister and I had meandered to school, sniffing and poking at pussywillows and ant hills, lay somewhere in the territory Big Bear and Wandering Spirit had roamed with their warriors just ahead of General Strange in May or June, 1885."[6] However, whereas Stegner is bitter about what was denied him as a child ("The very richness of that past as I discover it now makes me irritable to have been cheated of it then"[7]), Wiebe sees the process more positively: "in forcing me to discover the past of my place on my own as an adult, my public school inadvertently roused an anger in me which has ever since given an impetus to my writing" (*VL*, 134). To this essentially creative indignation we owe the novels about Big Bear and Louis Riel. Above all, once discovered, this past becomes a possession that is both permanent and precious. As Wiebe remarked at an interview, "it seemed to me that when I looked at the past of where I was at [*i.e.*, northern Saskatchewan] . . . there was as much past there as anywhere else in the world" (*VL*, 205). By recreating it, Wiebe has recovered it as a past for all of us.

But Wiebe is also a close and careful student of his own Mennonite past, and the exploration of this heritage found fruition in *Peace Shall Destroy Many* and especially in *The Blue*

Mountains of China. The former is a moving portrayal of the difficulties of maintaining Mennonite values in the modern world while the latter celebrates in the form of a saga-like chronicle some representative examples of their recent history. As a leading sociological historian of the Mennonites has written, "Mennonite history is determined not so much by a preconceived idea of a perfect society, but by the indefatigable search for a form of social life which would allow man to realize the ideal of a Christian life according to the Bible."[8] In Wiebe's third novel, the "blue mountains of China" become a potent if equivocal symbol of that search.

Wiebe's Mennonite background has been an obstacle to his acceptance within the mainstream of Canadian literature, since a large part of the Canadian reading public is ignorant of Mennonite principles and (not altogether without reason) suspicious of religious and didactic fiction. The relation between Wiebe and didacticism will be discussed later in the context of individual novels; suffice it to say here that Wiebe shares this unease ("I never consciously think of writing a so-called Christian novel. . . . If you are what you are, and what you're writing is any good, it's there anyway; you don't have to spell it out"[9]). When he is writing at his best, the religious attitudes are integral to the artistry of his fiction, transcending the sectarian to become probing and profound inquiries into the nature of human responsibility. None the less, the first point remains an unfortunate barrier; some elementary background concerning Mennonite history and beliefs is, if not essential, at least helpful.

Wiebe has himself provided a basic introduction in his foreword to *Peace Shall Destroy Many*. The Anabaptists, he notes there, were "the extreme evangelical wing of the Reformation movement," whose pacifist principles and insistence on the separation of church and state brought them into conflict with both the religious and secular authorities. Wiebe continues: "Like ancient Israel, they were a religious nation without a country. They were driven from Switzerland to America, from Holland and northern Germany to Prussia, then Russia, finally to North and South America. Wherever they went they carried peculiar customs, a peculiar language [Low German], a peculiar faith in the literal meaning of the Bible" (*PDM,* ix).

So much for basic history. But, because there are many kinds of Mennonites, and because in certain parts of Canada they are best known for old-fashioned clothes and outdated agricultural practice (characteristics that distinguish a section of Ontario Mennonites but not those of the prairies who came to Canada at a different time and by a different route), it may be useful to clarify Wiebe's own position. The earliest (and, for the most part, more conservative) of the prairie Mennonites emigrated from the Ukraine in the 1870s, and these are generally known as *Kanadier*. The others, reluctant at that time to give up their prosperity in southern Russia, waited until the effects of the communist revolution made themselves unambiguously felt before coming to the New World in the 1920s.[10] These later immigrants are known as *Russländer,* and many of them, including Wiebe's parents, belonged to a distinct sect, the Mennonite Brethren. This group originated in 1860 when a number of Mennonites in Molotschna Colony broke away from the Church in protest against what it considered moral and ethnical backsliding.[11] Francis has described the history of this group in Canada as follows:

> The brotherhood of Mennonite Brethren was officially introduced into the province [of Manitoba] in 1884, when Elder Heinrich Vogt [or Voth] of Minnesota paid his first visit. . . . But the movement did not greatly progress until the arrival of the Russländer refugees. . . . They were more broadminded than any other branch with regard to the use of English at church functions. At the same time, they were more insistent upon total abstinence from nicotine and alcohol, and emphasized high standards of personal conduct.[12]

More recently (and the point is important for an understanding of the Mennonite tensions within Wiebe's novels) they have developed the evangelizing, outward-looking aspects of Christian witness rather than fostering the traditional Mennonite view of themselves as a people set apart.

Wiebe's parents (whom he has described affectionately as "very simple, unworldly wise people"[13]) fought a losing battle against the Depression and the harsh geography of northern Saskatchewan, and after the Second World War moved down to another Mennonite community at Coaldale, Alberta. They were eager that at least their youngest child should receive a good education, and Wiebe eventually attended the University of Alberta as an undergraduate. On graduation he won a Rotary fellowship which enabled him to pursue his studies at the University of Tuebingen in West Germany, an experience that greatly expanded his horizons: "That year in Germany I saw another world, became more aware of the history of another place, and was able to see how my life was distinctive."[14] On his return he took a theology degree from the Mennonite Brethren Bible College in Winnipeg, and for eighteen months, from January 1962 to June 1963, he was the first editor of the *Mennonite Brethren Herald.* He succeeded in firmly establishing the magazine as a stimulating and challenging forum of Mennonite news and views before resigning after the controversy caused by the publication of his first novel. This incident did not, however, produce the separation that might have been expected. Wiebe has emphasized the wide "spectrum of attitude" within the Church, while admitting that, for him, "the meaning of being Mennonite Brethren is to be confused" (*VL*, 34). None the less, he has been able to pursue an independent path while remaining within the Mennonite Brethren, and may be said to speak for those Mennonites who attempt a middle road between the conservative extremes (represented by Deacon Block and his Wapiti community in *Peace Shall Destroy Many*, and, more congenially, by Frieda Friesen and the Sommerfelder group in *The Blue Mountains of China*) and the worldly-minded assimilationists who remain Mennonite only in name (and sometimes not even in name, like the Will[ia]ms family in the latter book). Although it would be false to speak in terms of mouthpieces, Wiebe clearly shares many of the attitudes of Joseph Dueck, the young teacher in *Peace Shall Destroy Many*, and sympathizes with John Reimer, who carries his cross along the Trans-Canada Highway in *The Blue Mountains of China*. His position involves a remarkable and by no means easy union of the modern and the traditional. As Wiebe expressed it in an interview with Donald Cameron: "I would like to think of myself as someone who's trying to live what the original Anabaptists were about. They're very contemporary, in a way, because they felt that the social structures that had evolved in the west had no sanction. To be an Anabaptist is to be a radical follower of the person of Jesus Christ."[15] It is at once a deeply sincere, challenging, and above all honourable position, firm but not stuffy, traditional without being in any way conventional.

As we look back at Wiebe's childhood and origins, we can recognize an almost inevitable logic in his development as an artist. His major contribution to Canadian literature consists in the creation out of his unique but at the same time curiously representative experience of a corpus of fiction that succeeds in relating the human past with that of the land. From the history of his own people, a history determined by the dynamic force of their religious beliefs, he has turned more recently to the history of western Canada where, as a result of the Mennonite diaspora, he himself was born. And he sees in this history a complement to the autochthonous religious instincts of Big Bear and the apocalyptic visions of Riel. History and religion are thus welded into his own fictional scheme.

Wiebe is adamant in his conviction that his aims could only be realized through the medium of fiction. He makes the point in a central and frequently quoted statement from his essay, "Passage by Land":

To touch this land with words requires an architectural structure; to break into the space of the reader's mind with the space of this Western landscape and the people in it you must build a structure of fiction like an engineer builds a

bridge or a skyscraper over and into space. A poem, a lyric,
will not do. You must lay great steel lines of fiction, break up
that space with huge design and, like the fiction of the
Russian steppes, build giant artifact. No song can do it; it
must be giant fiction.[16]

The transmutation of history into fiction, of action into word,
became Wiebe's overriding aesthetic challenge.

"Primitive peoples," he insists, "lay little or no stress on the
supposed difference between fact and fiction."[17] But if this is true
of Big Bear it is also true of the creator (or, rather, recreator) of Big
Bear. Wiebe has also argued that "the line between history and
fiction is an impossible line anyway."[18] The facts of history are
created out of human actions, and the scientific historian considers himself bound to stick as close to these facts as he can. But
Wiebe, who occupies a place closer than any of his novelist
predecessors to that of the professional historian, recognizes the
need to reunite the facts with their human origins. He is familiar
with what he calls "that passionate emotion that seizes a storyteller and will not let him rest until he has *made* something out of
facts" (*VL*, 217).

This "making" involves the discovery of the right viewpoint
from which the historical "facts" need to be seen. In *The
Temptations of Big Bear,* a shifting perspective was necessary.
The assumptions of the whites, whether official representatives of
government like Morris and Dewdney and Magistrate Hugh
Richardson or individuals caught up in the rebellion like James
Simpson and Kitty McLean, needed to be juxtaposed, often
violently, with those of the Indians. By contrast, *The Scorched-
Wood People* requires a different approach. Although we see the
Riel rebellions from all sides, the mediating vision is that of Pierre
Falcon, poet-singer of the Métis. The white historian has given
the white perspective often enough, but a resurrected Pierre
Falcon can place Riel within the context of his own people, can
force us to see the whole uprising through the eyes of those who
were impelled to take up arms. Wiebe's achievement is not merely

to comprehend this vision (the word is needed) in himself but to communicate it to others.

"What we have to do," Wiebe remarked during an interview, "is dig up the whole tradition, not just the white one. It's not a recorded tradition, it's a verbal one" *(VL,* 206). He knows also that "human understanding is tied to language."[19] Such observations remind us that, for all its complicated relation to facts, truth, and history, Wiebe's fiction depends for its ultimate success upon words. Words and, above all, voice. Where is the voice coming from? The title of one of Wiebe's short stories, which later became the title of the volume in which it was collected, is central to his work. It is a question we must ask, as I have implied in the previous paragraph, of *The Temptations of Big Bear* and *The Scorched-Wood People.* We ask it, too, of *The Blue Mountains of China,* where the speaker changes from chapter to chapter as different events and participants in the evolving Mennonite quest are introduced. Only if we can recognize and interpret the voice are we in a position to understand the issues at stake. But we find, if we begin to look more closely, that "voice" is a continuing preoccupation in his work. In an early chapter of *Peace Shall Destroy Many,* when a split appears to be opening between the "conservative" and "liberal" members of the Wapiti Mennonite Church, we find this: " 'Brother Dueck!' The Deacon's voice overwhelmed all, steel eyes flaming. Joseph's voice was snuffed, the sound and the look a bolt to blast everyone" *(PDM,* 60). Here the question at issue (as so often in Mennonite controversy) is language: the young teacher has spoken to the youth group in English instead of the customary High German. The matter is debated at a church meeting, the congregation exposed to speeches and rhetoric. Words, voice, language, speech: these are both key terms and key concepts. When Wiebe can write, a few lines later, "the silence was deafening" *(PDM,* 60), we sense a rough but palpable verbal originality in the author himself. Here we see Rudy Wiebe developing his own "voice," one that becomes stronger, more flexible, and more eloquent as his art matures.

In *First and Vital Candle,* the transitional novel in which

Wiebe develops many of his other fictional techniques, language and voice are less immediately conspicuous. None the less, the memorable scenes in the book include Oolulik singing her Eskimo songs during the blizzard that symbolizes the death of her people, the voices of the spirits in the Indian shaking-tent, and Josh Bishop's eloquent speech at the close of the war of words in the climactic scene at Bjornesen's store. It is, in fact, a novel in which the contrasts between passion and violence on the one hand and quietness and decency on the other are presented through the loud and soft voices of the chief protagonists.

Voice is, of course, integral to *The Blue Mountains of China*, not only in the different emphases and speech-rhythms of the varying narrators, but more centrally in the section entitled "The Vietnam Call of Samuel U. Reimer." In a scene ironically reminiscent of one in the Book of Samuel, Reimer hears the voice of God calling him to proclaim peace in Vietnam. This is a brilliant episode, poised between serious didacticism and a rather bitter and brittle humour, in which two of Wiebe's vital and recurring concerns, voice and peace, subtly coalesce. Moreover, the artistic effect of *The Blue Mountains of China*, when examined closely, is found to be essentially linguistic; it depends for its success on the skilful orchestration of numerous voices that narrate the disparate but ultimately unified incidents.[20]

When Big Bear is approaching the treaty-gathering in the first chapter of *The Temptations of Big Bear*, James McKay warns Alexander Morris, the lieutenant-governor: "Wait till you hear his voice" (*TBB*, 15). And his "gigantic voice" (*TBB*, 185) dominates the novel: "Big Bear's voice was a tremendous cry echoing over the valley" (*TBB*, 23). It fails him, however, in the crucial scene at Frog Lake where he shouts to his people to desist from massacre "but his great voice was lost in the immense lake and creek valley and the far hills" (*TBB*, 258). *The Temptation of Big Bear* resembles *The Blue Mountains of China* in that a total experience of the novel hears the voice of Big Bear in relation to many others, the narrative combining written records, oral testimony, and scenes reported through the eyes of both whites and Indians.

Similarly, *The Scorched-Wood People* opens with Riel hearing "Gabriel's voice boom in the next room" (*SWP*, 10). It is the first of many voices that speak to him in the course of the novel ("He once even told a reporter the voice from the flames spoke to him in Latin" [*SWP*, 140]). Moreover, the words applied to Riel's own voice—"his voice like thunder," "a tremendous voice," "the terrifying voice" (*SWP*, 187, 222, 223)—recall those used to describe Big Bear's. And just as Big Bear hears the "terrifying song" of his God (*TBB*, 182)—as, on another though very different level, did Samuel Reimer—so Riel derives his energy and power from what he believes to be the inspiration of a heavenly voice. Wiebe clearly recognizes an important connection between his religious preoccupations and his artistic concern for voice. The Biblical prophets, he claims, "had such great voices . . . [b]ecause they felt they spoke directly from God. They didn't speak out of the smallness of man, but out of the greatness of all that man can comprehend" (*VL*, 155).

In *The Mad Trapper,* his most recent work of extended fiction, the emphases are somewhat different. None the less, an eloquent contrast is established at the opening between the sounds of men in community (the dance at Fort McPherson) and the silence of the wilderness out of which Albert Johnson comes and into which he goes. And at the climax of the novella the sound of "Wop" May's Bellanca, combined with Frank Hersey's radio-communications, obtrudes into the Arctic waste and Johnson knows himself defeated by the noisy world of technological man.

The short story "Where is the Voice Coming From?" offers a paradigm of all the effects I have been discussing here. It is, ultimately, a story about writing a story. The subject is the death of Almighty Voice, the Cree outlaw shot by the police in 1897; the governing image of the story—and, I would argue, by extension, of the whole of Wiebe's work—is "his death chant no less incredible in its beauty than in its incomprehensible happiness":

And there is a voice. It is an incredible voice that rises from among the young poplars ripped of their spring bark, from among the dead somewhere lying there, out of the arm-deep pit shorter than a man; a voice rises over the exploding smoke and thunder of guns that reel back in their positions, worked over, serviced by the grimed motionless men in bright coats and glinting buttons, a voice so high and clear, so unbelievably high and strong in its unending wordless cry. (*WV*, 143)

Wordless because, as the narrator admits in the last line of the story, "I do not, of course, understand the Cree myself." The narrator focuses on his own difficulty in coming to terms with the story. He examines the tangible remains, the police-court facts: part of the skull of Almighty Voice, still preserved in a museum; a cannon said to have been used in the final encounter; the guardroom from which Almighty Voice once escaped; an enigmatic photograph identified as that of Almighty Voice.[21] But what haunts the narrator, because he knows that within it lies the secret, is the voice that he cannot understand.[22]

The narrator is not Rudy Wiebe, though he shares many of Wiebe's attitudes and actions in approaching the story. Just as Almighty Voice is heightened by Wiebe's art to become a "representative" (inadequate word, perhaps, but less inadequate than "symbol") of the mystery at the heart of life, so the brooding, haunted narrator is a representative not only of Wiebe but of all true artists. Wiebe has commented on the relation: "Not that all of the story as it now stands actually happened to me. Far from it. But I want you to feel that it did; and it *did*, to some story-teller who, if I had perfect wish-fulfillment at the moment of writing, I would be."[23]

Wiebe may be called a "difficult" novelist in the sense that he makes considerable demands on the reader. He assumes as a matter of course that we approach him with the same kind of attention and indulgence of initial obscurity that we are prepared to bring to, say, James Joyce or William Faulkner.[24] He is, I think, the first Canadian novelist to make such unequivocal demands, and I consider it an enormously heartening development in Canadian literature that he should do so. He brings to the novel as an art-form three of the major prerequisites for serious art: a respect for the dignity and scope of the genre; a versatility in technique and language that matches in artistry the ambitious nature of his subject-matter; his sense of the novel as a developing mode of intellectual and imaginative exploration. From *Peace Shall Destroy Many* to *The Scorched-Wood People,* a consistent and expanding development is discernible. The move from Thom Wiens in *Peace Shall Destroy Many,* a naive believer who must have his belief tempered in the heat of violence, passion, and bitter controversy, to Abe Ross in *First and Vital Candle,* a man in search of something to believe, one who is keenly aware of the nullity of free-thinking agnosticism, is a bold but artistically logical step. Then the expansion from the concerns of the Mennonites in *Peace Shall Destroy Many* and *The Blue Mountains of China* to the Indian world of *The Temptations of Big Bear,* an expansion from the history of his own people to the history of his land, from a formally Christian to a technically non-Christian but none the less visionary and all-embracing view of the world, is equally impressive. Most notably, the subject of *The Scorched-Wood People,* Louis Riel, seemed when announced an obvious—indeed, inevitable—development, yet I do not know of anyone who recognized this development while it was in process. Such is the nature of artistic, organic growth. The five novels to date, together with the short stories, the novella *The Mad Trapper,* and the play *Far As the Eye Can See,* exist not merely as individual works but as a substantial and coherent *oeuvre.* The growth of this corpus, and the technical methods developed to contain it, will be the subject of subsequent chapters.

2   *Peace Shall Destroy Many*

When *Peace Shall Destroy Many* first appeared in 1962, it provoked bitter controversy among Mennonites, but in Canadian literary circles it was greeted with respect as a fresh and challenging "problem novel." The story of Thom Wiens, torn between the faith and traditions of his Mennonite forefathers on the one hand and his own human instincts plus the demands of the non-Mennonite outside world on the other, provided a central narrative around which questions of national loyalty and religious principle, communal isolation and involvement, personal doubts and collective pressures, Christian ideals and modern values (or lack of them) could be explored and debated. Here was a work of fiction prepared to deal with serious and pressing issues. At the same time, it bore all the signs of a first novel. Readers coming upon the non-Mennonite schoolteacher's reference to Thom's "tremendous seriousness" (169) might well apply the phrase to the novelist himself. They would also detect self-consciousness—and, often, curious awkwardness—in the prose, a stiffness in the dialogue and a corresponding earnestness in parts of the argument; but it was not difficult to recognize a mastery of the two hallowed if old-fashioned novelistic virtues: a strong, sustained plot and sound, well-differentiated characterization.

Set in an isolated community in northern Saskatchewan, this problem novel appears at first sight to belong also within the regional category. The descriptive "preludes" that open the four seasonally-organized parts, numerous scenes portraying the daily life and labour on the farm (ploughing, hay-mowing, berry-picking, etc.), the presentation of a local group with its own attitudes and practices unfamiliar to the majority of the novel's readers, all these are the characteristic features of regional writing. Moreover, the introduction of two articulate outsiders, the Mennonite Joseph Dueck and the non-Mennonite Razia Tantamount, to provide connection with the outside world and a means of measuring the distinctive qualities of the community, is a conventional, even stale structural device in regionalist fiction.

But *Peace Shall Destroy Many*, while drawing upon elements in regionalism, is decidedly more ambitious in scope. Wiebe's hero endeavours to reconcile the old and the new, and the novel attempts a similar synthesis. Regional fiction invariably depends upon a balance between the peculiar features that distinguish a specific community or area and the connecting links that reveal the macrocosm within the microcosm. But the Mennonites have continually emphasized their separation from the rest of the world. In a passage strikingly relevant to *Peace Shall Destroy Many*, E.K. Francis has written:

> When the conservative party in the Mennonite colonies of Russia protested against the 'worldliness' of their brethren, they deplored as much their social mingling with outsiders as their adoption of the ways and institutions of this world. And when the most conservative of them turned to Canada, they fled from the world's inroad into their life in the Old Country to a place which seemed remote enough and isolated enough, both geographically and socially, to give hope that contact with the world could henceforth be avoided with greater success.[1]

But in *Peace Shall Destroy Many* this withdrawal is not so much an accepted norm as the subject for debate. As Allan Dueck has pointed out, "non-resistance . . . has in Wapiti come to mean noninvolvement,"[2] and the moral distinction between the two terms is crucial. The isolation of Wapiti is not a simplifying device but the basis for the novel's questioning. Should a community withdraw from the rest of the world? This raises an important moral problem. But Wiebe asks a more disturbing antecedent question: *can* a community withdraw from the rest of the world? Once the question is posed in these terms, *Peace Shall Destroy Many* transcends the categories of regional novel (this is what life is like at Wapiti) and problem novel (how should a pacifist respond if he is summoned for military service?) to reveal itself as a profound examination of human nature, human principle, and human conduct—in short, as a criticism of life.

The paradoxical title, from one of the visions in the Book of Daniel, raises an issue which becomes the prime concern not only of this novel but of the whole of Wiebe's work—the ironic connection between peace and violence. According to the official principles of the community, the Mennonites have withdrawn from a wicked and violent world to live the simple and honest life ordained by God. But this does not, of course, prevent the forces of violence from invading the quietness of Wapiti. In the first chapter, the clash is presented in its simplest form when military planes exercise in the skies over the community, breaking its tranquillity, and causing still births in the cattle. Peace belongs here, violence is there, yet the effects of violence are evident both here and there. For the young Thom Wiens the distinction is clear-cut, but the scene has effectively illustrated the impossibility of isolation: "Nowhere was there peace from them" (22).

Since *Peace Shall Destroy Many* is, among other things, a *Bildungsroman*, Thom will learn in the course of the novel that his simple dichotomy is inapplicable. In the baseball game in the second chapter, he comes to recognize the potential of violence within him. Later, as we learn of Deacon Block's early history in Russia, we realize that Wapiti is itself grounded in violence. Block, a powerful and well-drawn character at least as memorable as the more central Thom, had deceived his fellow-Mennonites in Russia and even killed while fighting for the life of his starving son; his leadership of the Wapiti community is generated by his determination to escape the temptation to violence, but it can never annul the tendency in his deepest self. At the end of the novel, Hank Unger, having left Wapiti to join in the violence of the outside world to which he is attracted, returns and provokes both Thom and Deacon Block's son to a savagery that has always existed below the surface. That Wapiti shares a tendency to violence with the rest of the world is now manifest to all. The ending is poised between a depressing exposure of guilt and a hopeful self-recognition.

But to describe the subject-matter of the book as the connections between peace and violence is not in itself sufficient. Like all novels of any importance, *Peace Shall Destroy Many* is about human relationships. We see the tendency towards violence not as an abstraction but as it manifests itself in Thom Wiens, Deacon Block, and Hank Unger; similarly, we see the psychological pressures of the dominant community ethic in specific instances as it affects Elizabeth Block ("Can't you see what's happened to me?" [141]), Herman Paetkau who is ostracized for marrying a Métis, and Thom Wiens once again as he comes to question the values and practices of the community. At its best (there are places, admittedly, where the novel falters because the author becomes too explicitly, and abstractly, didactic) *Peace Shall Destroy Many* deals not so much with ideas in themselves as with the impact these ideas have upon individuals.

A recurrent example of imperfect human relationships within the novel (especially interesting in the light of Wiebe's later fiction) involves the neighbouring Indian and Métis communities. In the first chapter, Thom rebukes his younger brother for swearing "like a half-breed" (15), and in the scene at the school picnic the uneasy relationship is made explicit: "Only a few Mennonites ever neared the Moosomin homestead, and they never went inside the four-walled shack or knew the mixture of common-law wives and husbands and children that were crammed there. Breeds lived as they lived: they were part of unchangeable Canada for the Mennonites" (31). When Thom participates in Sunday-school teaching, he meets opposition from his Church because, as he eventually realizes, the Mennonites do not want any development that would encourage further contact.[3] Herman Paetkau's action in living with and eventually marrying a Métis woman brings the matter to a head:

> Why should Herman not have married Madeleine? The reason lay painfully open now: she was a half-breed, and a Mennonite just did not marry such a person, even if she was a Christian. [Thom] stared at the bared thought. Despite this summer's work with the breed children every Sunday afternoon, he suddenly knew that he had not yet seen them as quite human. (110)

Later, Elizabeth Block's illicit sexual relation with Louis Moosomin (Madeleine's brother) becomes a bitter, ironic, almost parodic symbol of the human interconnection between Mennonites and their neighbours. In each case the point is made in terms of individual discovery—Thom's realization of his own prejudice, Elizabeth's instinctive response to an overpowering human need. One of the hopeful signs at the end of the novel is presented within the same pattern of reference. Thom is impressed by a scene in the school pageant (itself framed with hypocrisy and violence) in which the Métis Jackie Labret, acting one of the three kings, bent down "to lead the way to the manger" (237).

Peace Shall Destroy Many, then, is a novel of ideas, but emphasis must be laid not so much on "ideas" as on "novel." At the end of the book, Thom realizes that peace and violence are ultimately inseparable: "And in the heat of this battle lay God's peace" (238). But he has come to this understanding through experience that Wiebe has imbedded in the fictional structure of his novel. The climactic scene of violence in the barn parallels, in an apparently crude but in fact subtly effective way that reminds us of the principle of travesty by parallel employed in some of the medieval mystery-cycles, the pageant of the birth of the Prince of Peace in the manger at Bethlehem. Hal's innocent question,

"What happened in the barn?" (238), is a deeper question than he knows, as Patricia Morley has pointed out.[4] But Wiebe has enforced the point earlier when the adult Mennonites experience their epiphany in the barn, "staring at the tableau in the aisle" (236). The emphasis falls not on a detachable "message" but on the way that Thom has worked his way through to acknowledging the truth about himself. Wiebe is rightly uneasy at being called a "didactic novelist" since this too often implies a conspicuous teaching function. His values are integral to his novels, not imposed artificially upon them. As we look back at this first novel with an awareness of his subsequent work, it is the sometimes hesitant, sometimes bald, but often startlingly effective artistry that is most apparent.

"When I was writing my own first novel," Wiebe observed recently, "I had a sense that no one had ever written about what I knew and had lived" (*VL*, 215). The remark occurs in a sympathetic discussion of Frederick Philip Grove where Wiebe acknowledges his debt to the earlier Canadian novelist. Whatever Wiebe may have thought at the time, he now realizes the extent to which he was able to build upon Grove's example. Like Grove (whose first teaching positions in Manitoba were in Mennonite communities) he displays a sense of the high moral responsibility of the novelist's calling, a capacity to create memorably climactic scenes and, as we saw in the previous chapter, the ability to develop a consistent pattern over a series of novels. Indeed, one of the most interesting points to emerge from a study of Wiebe's development is the conviction that, with the possible exception of Margaret Laurence and her debt to Sinclair Ross, he is perhaps the first important Canadian novelist who has been able to benefit from a *Canadian* fictional influence. *Peace Shall Destroy Many* is continually recalling Grove. This is most obvious, perhaps, in the clash of generations, Thom and Joseph Dueck and Elizabeth Block on one side and Deacon Block and the elders on the other. Indeed, in the climactic scene when Elizabeth is found to be pregnant, Mrs. Block's insistence that she will leave her husband if he turns out the daughter inevitably recalls a scene in Grove's

Two Generations where Mrs. Patterson makes the same threat when taking the side of her children. Whether Wiebe had read *Two Generations* at the time his first novel was being written is uncertain and ultimately unimportant; the similarity is instructive because it points up a similar cast of mind in the two novelists.

Again, Razia Tantamount the schoolteacher has much in common with Clara Vogel in Grove's *Settlers of the Marsh,* even to the way in which her love of dances and use of cosmetics are offered as shorthand indications of her corrupted urban values. And Deacon Block, as I have already implied, is next in line to Grove's succession of authoritarian patriarchs. But the connections with Grove can be pushed further. Thom feels, like so many Grove heroes, that he was "working out God's promise that man would eat his bread in the sweat of his face" (12). The sharply drawn sides ("Was there only the old Block or the young Unger way?" [231]) also suggest Grove's moral dichotomies, especially in *Settlers of the Marsh,* and Thom's sexual naivety is not far from Niels Lindstedt's. More subtly, certain simple but profoundly effective details—I am thinking in particular of the appearance of Herman Paetkau and his Métis wife Madeleine at the funeral of Elizabeth Block as a suggestive image of Elizabeth's affair with the Métis Louis—indicate that Wiebe had learned even more from Grove's inconspicuous artistic procedures than he may have been aware of.[5]

Even some of Wiebe's apparent awkwardnesses resemble Grove's. The third chapter, in which Thom walks with Annamarie Lepp in the moonlight and they discuss war and pacifism, is generally criticized as a gauche and clumsily-conceived scene. The reader is most likely to regard it as a love-scene betrayed by the self-conscious embarrassment of the author. But Wiebe's intentions, like Grove's, are more complex than they seem, and they are achieved with a somewhat ponderous but not ineffective artistry. First, the uncertain clumsiness is at the very least as much Thom's as Wiebe's. Thom is as confused about his feelings for Annamarie as he is about his position concerning the war. Again,

Mennonite conventions strictly regulated the behaviour of the young and unmarried, and one of the central topics of the novel is the way in which Thom is pulled between the conflicting claims of traditional practices and challenging new ways. The youthful uncertainty in an unfamiliar situation is painful but deliberately and poignantly so.

What might be identified as the prime "meaning" of this scene is conveyed through Thom's action of throwing a stone into the gravel-pit to silence the frogs. At first, Thom is merely displaying his knowledge ("If you throw a stone into the water, they'll stop right away" [45]), but when he attempts the demonstration all but a deep-croaking frog near them continue undisturbed. Whatever significance the incident may have relates to Thom's unease about how to behave with Annamarie alone. He tries to show off with a display of knowledge, and he fails. But they go on to discuss pacifism, "alternative service" and the moral responsibility of the individual ("there comes a time when you must take a stand" [46]), and then the scene with the frogs is repeated:

> He arose slowly and, using his entire body in a flare of viciousness that spurted and died, flung a stone against the pool. But it did not splash. It skipped beautifully in its flatness, dropping gently with a final plop into a far gleam of water. His shoulder ached. A few frogs ceased, the rest croaked on. (47)

The "flare of viciousness" is one manifestation of the impulse towards violence which is so strong an undercurrent beneath the surface of the whole novel. But the throwing of the stone is now recognized as an emblem of the ineffectiveness of minority action. Thom's trivial attempt to silence the frogs becomes, as it were, a representative symbol of the much more important but equally doomed attempt to "take a stand" in the world war.

I have examined this scene in some detail because it is crucially representative as an example of the art of the younger

Wiebe. The scene is not without its weaknesses. The dialogue is stiff, a little too intense, and the inevitable contrast between the expected love-scene and the moral debate, however deliberate, remains unsatisfying. It may not be irrelevant to point out that intimate scenes between the sexes are often awkward in Wiebe (as they are in Grove); not until the scene between Riel and Marguerite in *The Scorched-Wood People* does a sense of authorial embarrassment totally disappear. But more important is the imagistic appropriateness of the frog scene, the way in which it communicates intellectual meaning beneath the level of plain narrative. This fumbling, rough-hewn but ultimately powerful artistry fits the tonal quality of the novel, and the effect is made possible, I believe, by a deep and individual response to Grove's fictional achievement.

One of the most fascinating features of *Peace Shall Destroy Many*, indeed, is the way in which we can watch an important novelist in the process of mastering his craft. At first sight the novel looks traditionally straightforward in its construction. The four-part seasonal division is obvious (though, again, appropriate for Wiebe's purpose here), and the relation between inner and outer weather is maintained throughout. "Perhaps man even had a spiritual winter," Wiebe tells us in the final part (199), forcing the analogy home. The image of storm that recurs, literally and metaphorically, until the whole narrative works up to the devastating outbreak of violence in the barn at the Christmas season is a related effect. But Wiebe also makes a number of technical experiments, the harvest of which is gathered in subsequent novels. In the fourth chapter, for example, the clash between old and new ways is debated at the church meeting, and we view this through Thom who, typically and appropriately, is swayed by both sides. Since we see through Thom's eyes during most of the novel, this is not in itself remarkable, but the scene is balanced in the eleventh chapter when the funeral of Elizabeth Block is presented, at least initially, from the viewpoint of the non-Mennonite teacher, Razia Tantamount. What in another novel by another novelist might have been offered sympathetically as a "human" response is here deeply shocking: "The sounds of the prayer tumbling past her ear in the stillness, she thought, What a body he must have under those outdated clothes!" (150) If it be objected that such an effect is crude, at least a partial justification is the fact that Razia is herself crude, that Wiebe is exposing a basic crudity in the attitudes of unbelieving, emancipated, worldly people like Razia who are pleased to think that they have outgrown the old-fashioned Mennonite notions and are moving in the vanguard of progress. A more sophisticated effect is not needed here, but in experimenting briefly with shifts in narrative perspective, Wiebe (we can now see) is rehearsing for more complex experimentation in his mature novels from *The Blue Mountains of China* onwards.

But the most radical technical experiment occurs in the eighth chapter. Here Thom, left at home while the church meeting is discussing the case of Herman Paetkau and his relation with Madeleine Moosomin, listens to a radio broadcast at the time of the liberation of Paris. Wiebe presents this chapter in a series of juxtaposed spliced sections; a direct transcript of the broadcast is continually interrupted by Thom's wandering thoughts as he relives the occasion several months before when he discovered Madeleine living in Herman's cabin. A contrast is set up between the contemporary symbol of "liberation" and the rigidity of the church to which Thom belongs. Both scenes involve deep incongruities: the soldier in the cathedral, the guns firing within the house of God in the one scene; the challenge to the community rules and the Métis woman excluded from the Church on the other. This is, of course, no clear-cut contrast. Thom is still confused, and the comparison between the two scenes can obviously lead to differing conclusions. Above all, the fact that the comparison involves a scene from the outside world, the world of godless violence, and one in the Mennonite community, the place of supposed peace, points up the serious irony at the heart of the novel.

Peace Shall Destroy Many is a young man's novel. Though not in itself autobiographical, it draws heavily on Wiebe's own experience. The Wiens family came from Russia to Canada in 1930 just like Wiebe's parents. Thom is considerably older than his creator—interestingly enough, the younger brother Hal is the one who corresponds in age to Wiebe himself. Wiebe is apparently working out imaginatively within the novel what his own situation might have been if he had been a few years older and so liable to military service. At the same time, Wiebe, like Thom, chafed against the restrictions of the traditional Mennonites and the writing of this novel seems to have been an imaginative testing of his own position within his Church as well as an independent artistic achievement.[6]

Stylistically, too, *Peace Shall Destroy Many*, with its curious blend of the conventional and the original, is recognizably apprentice work. Most readers (and reviewers) have noted an occasional murkiness in Wiebe's writing: ungainly sentences, grammatical oddities, obscurities—sometimes even misused words. These may be explained, as in the case of Grove, by the fact that English is not Wiebe's native tongue. At the same time, and once more the likeness to the younger Grove of *Over Prairie Trails* is apparent, we recognize a conscious stylistic aim. The descriptive prologues to each part clearly strive towards a heightened effect. Individual sentences, often at the opening of chapters or sections, employ a conspicuously "poetic" prose ("On the fringe of day balanced the sun. The July world lounged clean as a washed cat." [66]). In this novel, especially, the use of striking and unusual similes is conspicuous; these are often effective in themselves, but not always clearly appropriate to the context. Individual words are frequently used in original ways that enforce metaphorical connections ("he could not lever his mind to reason" [41]; "the scene of the previous night aggressed across his memory" [137]). To argue that the novel's prose style imitates the clash between traditional acceptance and individual originality in the protagonist might well lead to over-subtlety and special pleading. The fact remains, however, that the Mennonite emphasis on truth and simplicity has not encouraged the emergence of imaginative Mennonite literature. Mennonite suspicion of fiction is well documented. Peter Klassen recalls "a fairly strong conviction that Kunst (the fine arts) was largely under the control of the devil," E.K. Francis points out that "fiction and poetry were more rarely represented [than history, travel books, and other non-fiction] in a typical Mennonite library," and Wiebe himself has recently referred to "the lies my parents often told me I was reading in story books."[7] The stylistic unevenness of *Peace Shall Destroy Many* is probably not a conscious attempt to suit the action to the word, the word to the action; but it may well reflect tensions within the author of which the novel is itself both a product and an illustration.

When the book first appeared, Wiebe was editor of the *Mennonite Brethren Herald.* The controversy arising from its publication led to his resignation. Journalistic commentators on Wiebe have made much of this incident, and Wiebe himself has called it "a fantastic ruckus"[8]; but it is a mistake, I believe, to interpret it in black-and-white terms as a blatant example of conservative Mennonite prejudice. True, a number of Mennonites strongly disapproved of the novel's publication on the grounds that it constituted an exposé, an indictment of Mennonite hypocrisy deliberately offered to the outside world. (One thinks of Deacon Block's complaint to Joseph Dueck at the church meeting: "You criticized the church before *that* group?" [60].) This is not in fact an accurate description of the novel, but it is by no means an inaccurate forecast of the way in which the novel could, and would, be read. Here, for example, is one recent summary: *"Peace Shall Destroy Many* is a penetrating, remorseless analysis of the hypocrisies of Mennonite life that exposes cruelty, indifference, and hate beneath the mask of brotherly love."[9]

This is, of course, a distortion of Wiebe's intention. His basic point concerns the nature of human beings—*all* human beings. Joseph Dueck's remark at the church meeting, "We Mennonites, every one of us, are not better than other men" (62), proves decidedly double-edged. Wiebe is not saying, "this is what Mennonites are like," but rather, "this is what *even* Mennonites are like." He uses the Mennonite community as an example, partly because it is the one he knows best, partly because the hypocrisies and abuses show up more dramatically in such a context, but he is primarily offering the story as representative of human weakness and imperfection.[10] To confine its application to the Mennonites is to ignore the numerous references to the rest of the world—to the war, to the Russians, to Canadian militaristic pressures, to the "liberated" values of Razia Tantamount for whom *The Sun Also Rises* serves as a modern substitute for the Mennonite Bible (169). Once again, we discover that *Peace Shall Destroy Many* is a larger, more ambitious and, in the best sense of the word, more radical work than first appears. Though more traditional in form, it raises issues as universal and as generally applicable as those explored in Wiebe's subsequent novels.

Wiebe has never written another novel as conventionally structured, as "well-made" as this, but the organic development of his later fiction can be traced from this first book. The following passage, for example, must have conveyed comparatively little to readers in 1962, but we now see it as containing the seeds of *The Temptations of Big Bear* and *The Scorched-Wood People:*

When Herman mentioned that [Madeleine] was, on her mother's side, the great-granddaughter of Big Bear, of whom Thom had never heard, the woman had spoken softly and without show until the sunlight paled on the snow in the brief afternoon. She told of the great Indian who had ruled the Plains Cree as a true monarch; who had signed the treaty with the white man and given up a territory as great as many European countries; who, in his old age, could not prevent his blood-maddened warriors from massacring nine white men at Frog Lake because they believed that the Great White Mother had betrayed their contract. Hearing her tell of Big Bear, Louis Riel, Wandering Spirit, Thom glimpsed the vast past of Canada regarding which he was as ignorant as if it had never been. (111)

This epiphany is, one feels, Wiebe's as well as Thom's, and the passage indicates the direction of his development.

At this time, however, Christianity had a prior claim to his attentions. He had not yet recognized the possibility of artistically merging his Christian and historical interests. In Thom Wiens he had portrayed a thinking Christian who, while challenging some of the narrower beliefs of his forebears, had come to consider at least the possibility of a godless world:

> He could not deny that something had crashed within him. In the past six months he had questioned [Block's] every act: surely his own Christian faith should not now be affected. But the one log that held the jam had been jarred and he could sense within him the numb void that remained after the rush had vanished. (219)

In his next novel, Wiebe explores the opposite experience, taking as his protagonist a man who, having long since lapsed into an uncaring agnosticism, finds himself impelled towards a quest for something in which to believe. The innocent Thom Wiens gives place to the dissatisfied man of experience, Abe Ross in *First and Vital Candle*.

3   *First and Vital Candle*

In any writer's development the second novel is well known to be crucial. If he is not to become known as *homo unius libri*, the author of a successful first novel must demonstrate that he has not exhausted the pressing (and often personal) material that led him to attempt fiction in the first place. He must tap further creative resources, extend his range, build upon the experience already gained—above all, perhaps, improve his artistic discipline.

First and Vital Candle is the least known of Rudy Wiebe's novels. Although it was subsequently adapted for radio, this novel first published in 1966 was not reprinted until 1979. The original reviews were mixed and, although often respectful, never enthusiastic. At the time, it might well have been thought that Wiebe had failed to exploit his initial success with *Peace Shall Destroy Many*, but such assumptions would have been mistaken. As we shall see, criticisms can be brought against the book readily enough, but it represents none the less a remarkable advance without which the emergence of a mature novelist from *The Blue Mountains of China* onwards would not have been possible. Irrespective of its own merits, which are considerable, Wiebe needed to write this novel to complete his fictional apprenticeship. More than one reviewer used the word "old-fashioned" in connection with *First and Vital Candle*.[1] Such a judgment can be defended if confined to matters of theme and didactic argument, but it proves hopelessly off-target if fictional technique and creative invention are considered. Though no one is likely to claim it as Wiebe's best book, a case could be made for it, in retrospect, as his most auspicious one. The creative leap is in the process of being taken; once it is completed, the later novels become feasible.

At first sight, however, the link backward to *Peace Shall Destroy Many* is more evident. Abe Ross, the central character here, is Thom Wiens's shadow figure. Whereas Thom is engaged in a struggle with doubt, Abe fights against religious faith and acceptance. While Thom, by reason of his ancestry and upbringing, is presented as a sheltered and unworldly figure, Abe embodies a recognizably modern, "existential" consciousness. Thom is tied uneasily to his family and its traditions, to his roots in the past; at the opening of *First and Vital Candle* Abe, who has made a bold but crippling break from his, is completely (and, we soon realize, symbolically) alone. Thom is a naive idealist; Abe has reached a nullity beyond despair. Yet there are at the same time decided resemblances. Both long for an elusive peace but are forced to acknowledge the violence within themselves. Both recognize their loneliness not only as deprivation but also as challenge. Both are dissatisfied with mere· existence and find themselves engaged in an unending search for a set of values that can be not only admired but lived.

I have emphasized the connections between Thom and Abe because, even when they invite contrast rather than comparison, they point to a vital continuity. But there is a sense in which *First and Vital Candle* is much bolder in conception. In *Peace Shall Destroy Many* we can see Wiebe's own not altogether certain attitudes split between the assured Joseph Dueck and Thom Wiens with all his doubts and perplexities. Yet the intellectual viewpoint of the novel is still contained within the Mennonite community; the forces representing the outside world, even Razia Tantamount whose inner thoughts are briefly reproduced, remain apart from the moral centre of the book. In *First and Vital Candle*, the basic pattern is repeated, authorial sympathy clearly split between the nonsectarian missionary at Frozen Lake, Josh Bishop, and the dominating central figure of Abe Ross. But Abe, as I have indicated, is far more than a doubting Thomas; he has discarded all his spiritual beliefs and is struggling to maintain the moral code that they once accompanied. Josh's religious principles correspond to Wiebe's (his attitudes towards Jesus and pacifism, though allegedly independent of any specific Church, are recognizably Mennonite) but one also senses that in Abe's numbed lack of belief and response the author is exploring a state of mind he can imagine as possible within himself. And the scope of the novel is correspondingly extended. Whereas Thom's experience is limited to Wapiti, Abe knows the twin loneliness of city and wilderness, and he has been a participant in the war that is only a remote and unknown horror for Thom. The book takes account, as *Peace Shall Destroy Many* did not, of the broadening of Wiebe's experience of life in and immediately after his student years. This novel differs from its predecessor in that it is not in any sense a *Bildungsroman;* Abe's is an adult's search taking its point of departure in an adult's need.

In the ninth chapter Josh Bishop gives Abe an accurate description of himself: "a kind moral decent man but you haven't dared believe in anything except maybe yourself" (172). Much later Sally Howell, the schoolteacher with whom Abe falls in love, says of Alex, one of the Indians: "he lost the beliefs of his people and found nothing to replace them" (313). The parallel is striking, and points to one of the major structural effects in the novel that I shall discuss later. In a sense Abe represents "the whiteman's care-nothing road" (172) down which the Indians are plunging, or being plunged, and although he realizes its inadequacy, he finds difficulty in turning back. His view of life is chillingly presented in the following passage:

> . . . he sat on the bed-edge and stared down the naked length of his body. A slow, sardonic smile formed at his lip-corners: empty room, empty body, to be lived in as necessary and then left, no mark to betray who or what inhabited it, nothing

personal, human, left behind; when left, left completely like the husk of an insect that has long contorted and at last thrown off the hampering for what instinct tells it will be perfection at last. But he had no instinct for perfection, no belief for metamorphosis. Only nothing: so he had told himself for so many godawful years. (260)

Clearly, then, Abe Ross stands for modern man; his story cries out, in fact, for an allegorical reading. Having run away from his father (who bears an interesting resemblance to Deacon Block) and the restrictiveness of a narrow and empty extreme-Presbyterian home, he has no tolerance for the platitudes of Christian orthodoxy—"all the gibberish from precisely acted ritual to shapeless hallelujah-amen-ism, from idiotic appeals of emotion to as idiotic appeals of philosophy, from time-marking silence to banshee screams, with all the innumerable gradients of emotional and mental atrophy and massage between" (93). Wiebe is obviously not resting content with his own Mennonite position; one senses a determination to avoid any possible categorizing of himself as "religious" or "Christian" novelist.

When we first see Abe Ross (and he is the central consciousness of the novel, always present), he is an aimless wanderer in a modern city, out of place, uneasy, uncertain of his future—above all, lonely. He is, in Robert Frost's phrase, "one acquainted with the night." His following of an unknown woman until she disappears into an apartment building in the suburbs is a pathetic presentation of human need and modern isolation; if we read it with a knowledge of Wiebe's short stories, however, our reaction may well approach terror rather than pathos since we can faintly recognize a situation which, with only a slight psychotic slant, could merge into the tone of "Did Jesus Ever Laugh?". Once again, the supposedly Christian novelist is dealing with states of mind and patterns of experience that are anything but traditional or "old-fashioned."

The second chapter projects the lonely man into "sophisticated" urban society (a new territory for Wiebe). Meeting a school friend at a concert, Abe is taken to a fashionable party where his separation from conventional social *mores* becomes painfully evident. His attempts to explain the nature of Eskimo life to a gathering of the supposedly educated and enlightened, who can only respond with superficial clichés about the primitive and a taste for sexual innuendo, at one and the same time express Wiebe's own comment on contemporary values and indicate Abe Ross's representative dilemma. He is both part of and alienated from the society in which he finds himself. Entranced by the concert performance of Bach's St. John's Passion (an indication of his receptiveness to the spiritual), he is precipitated, only partly against his will, into small talk and smart trivia. Even the German harpsichordist's account of killing a Russian soldier during the war creates no more than a momentary serious response, which is dissipated almost at once in stale America-versus-Russia political argument. Moreover, the Bach soloist can make his living only by satisfying popular taste ("Dance hall music—jazz—that is the only—safe—music for me now" [38]), and the party, whose members had momentarily become "a congregation" in the concert hall (25), finds its own level by turning into a jazz-session—in which Abe drunkenly joins. Wiebe is writing in a powerfully realistic mode here, yet we are aware that Abe recognizes his true situation in hell. As Jim MacLaren remarks, guiding Abe towards a select group in the basement, "the real McCoy's downstairs" (24).

A trader employed by the Frobisher Company, Abe has recently witnessed a series of disasters in the Arctic that have left him depressed and despairing.[2] The chapter devoted to Oolulik, later published by Wiebe as a separate short story, is a moving account of survival and the failure to survive, of the inadequacy of white values, including religious values, in a grim and alien environment. Her death, a climax to the decimation of her tribe, haunts the rest of the novel just as it haunts Abe's moral consciousness. At the opening of the book Abe is looking for "some place that'll work me like a dog so I can lose all this trailing me and do something for somebody or something—at least forget" (95). He seems to be seeking a kind of secular retreat, and is sent (providentially, one is tempted to say) to an Indian community in northern Ontario, Frozen Lake, where an independent trader, the demonic Bjornesen, is corrupting the Indians with drinking sessions leading to greater excesses that end, as we learn much later, in "serial rape" (314). Here the forces of good and evil are locked in conflict, the former represented by the missionary Josh Bishop and the teacher Sally Howell. Abe, aligned with them on humanistic and moral grounds, cannot accept the religious basis for their position. The tension of the novel moves back and forth between concern for the Indian community and for the soul-state of Abe Ross himself.

A morality-play structure is discernible, then, just below the surface of the book. Although Abe is a distinct and convincing character, on one level of significance he is offered, allegorically and perhaps somewhat reductively, as a modern Everyman, and the external conflict at the appropriately named Frozen Lake has its psychological correspondence within his divided consciousness. Similarly, many of the characters who appear in the book take on an additional relevance in their relations to Abe. Thus Jim MacLaren, the schoolfriend, in his easygoing attitudes, his pattern of marriage and divorce, his relative crudity, is an example to be avoided; Oolulik the Eskimo woman, for whom "there is nothing left to believe" (82), represents a state disturbingly close to his own possible destiny; Kekekose, the Indian leader whose conversion to Christianity is curiously intertwined with Abe's own experience and response, serves as both comparison and contrast; even Josh Bishop, in the infuriating consistency of his Christian behaviour, is an index of Abe's moral if not religious commitment, a yardstick against which Abe measures and judges himself. I do not wish to suggest a rigid, systematic, allegorical pattern, but the presence of a level of meaning beneath that of surface realism needs to be constantly borne in mind.

Much of the effectiveness but also much of the difficulty in the novel stems from the presence of these different levels. The reader is constantly being required, as it were, to change gears, to move quickly and readily from one literary convention to another, and Wiebe does not always succeed in smoothing out the transitions. The book contains strong scenes of suspense (the confrontation in Bjornesen's store, the abortive attempt to rescue Sally), extended passages of moral and religious argument during which the narrative is suspended, and Abe's flashbacks into memories of personal crisis which, though essential to his own story, are remote from that of Frozen Lake. And overlying the whole, inevitably suggested by the religious element integral to the novel, we recognize a further allegorical or even anagogical dimension in which Sally's death is aligned—a little too easily, we may feel—to Christ's sacrifice and Abe's story is assimilated into an archetypal human pattern.

We should not, however, mistake this pattern. Abe changes in the course of the novel, and there is a sense in which *First and Vital Candle* is a book about change. Kekekose, "the old man [who had] found the strength to change" (325), becomes an example if not a model for Abe. And another Indian, James Sturgeon, remarks: "I did not know that that was what change was till [Josh Bishop] told me" (326). Yet Abe's progress is different. It is certainly not the conventional one within Christian tradition from sin to repentance or from opposition to conversion. Abe cannot, like Kekekose, embrace a new faith through the symbolic act of baptism. His personal situation may in certain respects be analogous, but it is uniquely his own. In the last pages he succeeds in achieving a credible positive that is the opposite of easily won. In its distinctive way, however, it does suggest the sanctioned pattern of mystical experience: utter desolation, the personal dark night of the soul, followed by—not union with the divine (that would be both inappropriate and impossible)—but an acceptance of possible meaning within apparent meaninglessness, the capacity to make a new start from a position of strength rather than weakness, something at least more hopeful than "the vacancy of all lone dangling humans" (352). Not a triumph, certainly not a miracle, but an emotional, psychological, and spiritual release.

At this point, the significance of the title becomes evident. A quotation from one of Gerard Manley Hopkins's sonnets, "The Candle Indoors" ("Mend first and vital candle in close heart's vault"), it alludes to the presence of a living flame in the depths of the self. Sally Howell, for whom Abe comes to feel a love that proves the existence of such a flame within him, uses the image while describing her own conversion: "It's more like a small flame starting which you can't snub. . . . It's an act of grace, complete irrefutable grace from God, catching fire in you, and it's real" (290). Ultimately Abe comes to recognize (and I would not make the point more emphatically than this) that for him God may be working through Sally: "he understood that this spot [her grave] would never again be of absolute importance to him because all that she had been and promised to be was flickering, alive in him" (354). It is important, I think, to stress that this is not a novel that tries to enforce a simplistic form of uplift. The final chapter, in which Sally is found dead, opens: "If there was a God, it was his act" (333). And Josh is prepared to admit: "Belief that God is opens you to the worst of all temptations: to detest him in helplessness" (348); at the end Abe knows that the life he still has to live will be "hardly less fearful" (354). The candleflame is uncertain and vulnerable, but it gives off light.

While discussing *Peace Shall Destroy Many*, I was able to separate the thematic aspects of the novel from Wiebe's artistic presentation of them. As the last paragraphs have indicated, this is hardly possible in *First and Vital Candle*, where the relation between the situation at Frozen Lake and Abe's psychological state is far subtler than the corresponding relation between Wapiti and Thom Wiens. For Wiebe as for Hopkins, the essential candle is "indoors," and he needs to draw on additional artistic methods to communicate Abe's momentous inner struggle. The more "modern" consciousness of Abe Ross must be explored with more appropriately "modern" fictional techniques.

The stylistic change from *Peace Shall Destroy Many* to *First and Vital Candle* is evident enough in the opening paragraphs of the novels. The descriptive "Prelude" in the first novel begins as follows:

> The school stood at the crossroads in the valley, its loggish
> face southward. Flanked by teacherage and sagging barn, it
> waited with its door yawning in the spring morning as the
> children neared on four roads cut like slashes through the
> bush. Reluctantly they came, listening tò the spring frog-
> song, touching the buds on the slim poplars, snuffing the
> freshness. Soon the yard rang with their running shouts and
> tumbled hills' re-echo. (*PDM*, 9)

One can sense here a deliberate attempt at "fine writing," the
young novelist's self-conscious aim to command a style. The
"loggish" face of the barn and the "tumbled hills" are evidence of
a palpable if somewhat idiosyncratic feeling for stylistic effect.
This is a prose that draws attention to itself. "Flanked by
teacherage and sagging barn" catches a visual image but approx-
imates dangerously to the rhythms of poetry, while the pathetic
fallacy of "waited" and "yawning," the last word rhyming
intentionally (one assumes) but also gratingly with "morning,"
points to a youthfully vigorous but as yet not fully disciplined
response to the emotive force of words and rhythms extending
beyond basic meaning.

The opening of *First and Vital Candle* shows no signs of
being written by the same author:

> He had been walking along Portage Avenue for more than
> an hour, glance searching out first a store window, then a car
> gliding by under throttled power, looking intensely though
> come the evening's end and dropping into bed he would
> remember not one detail of the mass, couples chatting as they
> passed oblivious, when looking down into a restaurant
> below street level Abe Ross saw the girl seated alone at a
> table. (9)

I am not arguing that this is better prose—there are a number of
awkward changes of direction resulting in grammatical strain
and inviting complaints about "fractured syntax" that early and

unsympathetic reviewers of Wiebe's work frequently registered[3]—but it is unquestionably different. The jerky, blurred effect is, of course, both intentional and appropriate. We are immediately propelled into the action; because we see it through the unfocused and preoccupied eyes of the as yet unidentified protagonist, we experience his sense of bewilderment and disorientation in the middle of an unfamiliar and alien city. The author has plunged both his character and ourselves into the midst of his fictional world (a process he will develop further in later novels), and is offering fluctuating impressions of representative modern life rather than a formal artistic composition. Though conventional third-person narrative is employed, an individual viewpoint continually cuts across it. The double perspective so important to the novel is established immediately.

An early reviewer objected to the novel's "architecture—or rather its lack of good architecture";[4] this now seems a strange remark since further examination reveals the book to be constructed with unusual care. It is divided into seven parts, and of these parts 1, 3, 5, and 7 are told by a third-person narrator limited to Abe's consciousness. Parts 2, 4, and 6, however, consist of first-person flashbacks. This is an unusual arrangement (the best-known example in English-language fiction is Dickens's *Bleak House*, though the relation between the two modes of story-telling is not so regular there), and the characteristic "feel" of *First and Vital Candle* is dependent upon it. Moreover, since part 2 recounts the recent tragedy of the Eskimos, part 4 a combination of university and army experience, and part 6 his leaving home in his teens, Abe is as it were urged by circumstances further and further back into his past in order to understand his present.[5]

These flashbacks, indeed, offer us a clue to the imagistic organization of the whole. The death of the Eskimos in the ice looks forward to the death of Sally near Frozen Lake; part 4, in which the two incidents presented are linked by the theme of bathing, carries undertones suggestive of baptism; part 6, containing the father's Old Testament curse, recalls Bjornesen's Indian one. Elements of past and present consistently interconnect. Indeed, the novel is meticulously planned throughout; the early chapters set in Winnipeg are filled with images and references that anticipate the moral and religious issues that Abe must face by the end of the book. The story of the iceberg and the ship, for instance, which Abe tells to the boy in the restaurant, provides an image of Abe's godless universe of destructive power, and a proleptic hint of Sally's death, yet, as Patricia Morley has pointed out, the iceberg ultimately proves the salvation of the ship's company and so may be interpreted as "a prophecy concerning the resolution of Abe's quest."[6] More obvious is the "incredible worship" (25) represented by Bach's St. John's Passion, to which I have already alluded. Others include the "Jesus saves" sign (20), the Gideon Bible in Abe's hotel room (41), the graffito scrawled on the bridge ("God be merciful to me a siner" [44]), the cathedral in which he sits and notices the plaque in memory of four who died by drowning (47). What seem at first sight casual, innocent details eventually take their place in a purposefully organized design.

Words recur as well as images, and most important among these are references to "breaking" and related actions. Together they lead up to the ambivalent climax. "Things are coming to a head," Sally notes prophetically; "Josh feels this winter something will break and so we're going there [Brink Island] for some days of prayer" (212). Neither Sally nor Josh, however, will help Abe "in trying to break any human being," even the evil Bjornesen, and Abe considers that to pray is merely "holding up fingerdabs of decency against a flood" (222-3). Later, "something had to crack" (254); "in the south the ice was softening, soon breaking" (259). Sally is confident, just before her death, that "the evil at Frozen [Lake] is opened at last" (281). At the climax, the breaking of the ice at the moment of baptism, the Indians' formal acceptance of Christianity—their spiritual rebirth coinciding, as we soon realize, with the physical death of Sally—is symbolically apt, but too neat to be fully convincing at the realistic level. The allegorical significances (signalled earlier by the "three-day rain" [309] and Abe's entering "the obviously empty room" [310], and underlined by Sally's christologically appropriate age [312]) become too insistent and conspicuous. The climax seems engineered in the wrong sense, manipulated to make a point; it is likely to strike us as artificial even if we recognize it as integral to the novel. And there can be no question, I think, that it *is* integral. The last manifestation of "breaking," as I have implied in the earlier discussion, is at least the beginning of the breakdown of Abe's resistance to Sally's religious view of the world.

At this point, perhaps, we can begin to isolate the peculiar difficulty that lies at the heart of the novel. In *First and Vital Candle* we find the clumsiness as well as the excitement of growing powers that may be considered characteristic of a transitional work. Here the conspicuous structuring of the climax seems in conflict with the modernist sense of tentative development that distinguishes Abe Ross's story. Elsewhere the didactic sections of the novel become oppressive; while they can be defended intellectually, they remain vulnerable artistically. Indeed, they are even more conspicuous here than in *Peace Shall Destroy Many*, partly because they are more blatantly imposed upon the narrative. The disputants seem too conveniently matched. In the second chapter, Granger is too crudely American, too extreme a parody, to be more than an argumentative token; and in the thirteenth, the Air Force officer Marsden (whose name, as Patricia Morley has observed, deliberately recalls the god of war[7]) appears to be literally flown in to Frozen Lake in order to argue the militarist position in the pacifism debate. None the less, although these didactic scenes become tiresome, they are in no way digressive. Wiebe is not merely attaching moral meanings on to a wilderness adventure; Abe needs these discussions to come to terms with the problems in his life. But Wiebe has not yet succeeded in fusing meaning and action; he only achieves this in the novels from *The Blue Mountains of China* onwards.

There are other difficulties. The scene at Kekekose's conjuring in chapter eight, where Abe's revolver is mysteriously (miraculously?) recovered from a river-bottom ten miles away, is a conspicuous example. Most of us share Abe's skepticism, yet, since it is a *donnée* in the story, we have to accept the conjuror's magical powers against all our preconceptions. Although Wiebe can cite anthropological evidence to justify the incident,[8] and despite the fact that he wants us to share the challenge to Abe's rationalist assumptions, the reader can be forgiven for considering it an infringement of the novelistic rules. If the author can require us to accept this, there seem no limits to his powers. Later, when Sally refers to the incident as an example of "outside kind of miracles [which] don't work any more" (284), we may understand its position within the intellectual framework of the book but this does not alter our sense of its representing an aesthetic intrusion.

In her study of Rudy Wiebe and Hugh Hood, Patricia Morley stresses the mythic patterns in their work. I am not convinced, however, that their presence is necessarily an artistic strength. For instance, she describes Bjornesen as "a mythic rather than a realistic character, . . . something out of Old Norse myth. When Bjornesen laughs, the earth shakes."[9] The point needs to be developed. In *First and Vital Candle*, the dimensions of saga, myth, or epic are imperfectly assimilated into the novel; once again, Wiebe's mastery of this aspect of his art only reveals itself in the later novels. Here, for example, Bjornesen's evil is never explained; it is a *donnée*, like Kekekose's magic, and must be accepted without question. Bjornesen is not a rounded character like Deacon Block, and we see him only as an embodiment of the powers of darkness. When, at the close of the novel, he shows signs of a growing humanity, this is comprehensible at the level of parable but unconvincing (because unprepared for) in terms of novelistic realism. Once again, the different levels in the fiction fail to cohere.

But it would be unfair to conclude a discussion of *First and Vital Candle* on a negative note. The faults are palpable enough, yet although they remain evident they matter less at each re-reading. More conspicuous, as we explore the novel again with an awareness of its overall shape, is Wiebe's rapidly expanding range of interest and insight, and the parallel growth of his technical capacities. The penultimate chapter, in which the speeches of Kekekose, James Sturgeon, and Josh Bishop are interspersed with Abe's memories of Sally and the restatement of his religious doubts, can be seen as an extension of the method employed in the eighth chapter of *Peace Shall Destroy Many* where the broadcast of the liberation of Paris cuts across Thom Wiens's troubled consciousness. Here Wiebe is manipulating his material creatively; we recognize the presence, to use his own terminology, not merely of a story-teller but of a story-*maker.* In the climactic scene of confrontation in Bjornesen's store and in the final pages in which Abe recognizes the flickering of the vital candle amid the shattering of his hopes, we can appreciate an amplitude of effect that threatens to break the bounds of this particular novel and goes far beyond the imaginative boundaries of *Peace Shall Destroy Many.* In such effects, epic fiction—or, in Wiebe's own phrase, "giant fiction"—may not be fully achieved but it is shown to be achievable. From the fitful manifestations of imperfectly developed powers here it is not an unduly surprising progression to the full-scale accomplishment represented by *The Blue Mountains of China.*

4　The Blue Mountains of China

With this third book Wiebe becomes a major novelist. Exceptional promise has evolved into indisputable achievement. We no longer have the sense that the writer is feeling his way towards the mastery of his craft. In particular, the earlier problem of reconciling his moralism with his literary artistry is solved. Didacticism is transformed into vision; what he has to say is now almost completely fused with how he says it. Above all, the tentative and exploratory tone of the earlier novels is replaced here with an assured confidence. The sensitive reader will recognize, within the texture of the writing, what I can only describe as the exhilaration of accomplishment.

The Blue Mountains of China, then, is an immensely rewarding novel, but by the same token it is also a very difficult one. Wiebe has now earned the right to make considerable demands upon his readers, and the book has to be read slowly and deliberately if its unique qualities are to reveal themselves. "I'm not for speed-readers," Wiebe has insisted.[1] More a saga than a conventional novel, the book recounts the stories of individual Mennonites which, when combined, form the representative epic-story of a whole people. It is a Christian odyssey in which we see the Mennonites wandering in a modern wilderness ever in search of a promised land of peace and religious tolerance symbolized by the evocative but elusive image that gives the book its title. This quest extends over many decades and several continents. We move from one generation to another, backward and forward in time, to and fro between old and new worlds. The mental agility of the reader is tested throughout.

After my own first reading of the novel, I was left, I remember, with a phantasmagoria of dimly-recognized, shadowy figures always in movement—alone on the march, alone on the run, but together on an endless epic journey across the spaces of the earth. But I also remember an experience of almost breath-taking power, a realization that here was a novelist with a breadth of vision, seriousness of purpose, and (above all) a dazzling artistry—qualities which are the hallmarks of a major writer. With each re-reading the shadows have receded, the outlines have grown clearer, the larger structural concerns have become more evident, and my admiration and appreciation have steadily grown.

More recently, with the publication of *The Temptations of Big Bear* and *The Scorched-Wood People,* Wiebe has acquired a deserved reputation as an "epic" novelist, and this designation first becomes possible with the appearance of *The Blue Mountains of China* (though, as I have indicated, signs of interest in epic material are present in *First and Vital Candle*). This is a story not merely of individual Mennonites but of the Mennonites as a people. It is a saga of endurance and a religious odyssey all in one. Wiebe is dealing with sets of people in different countries who are linked by common beliefs and a common purpose. But they are linked also, of course, by human weakness and suffering.

Moreover, the patterns of classical epic-story continually blend into a preoccupation with even larger Biblical structures. Throughout the book we are aware of an analogy between the Mennonites of the last few centuries and the ancient Israelites in the wilderness in the opening books of the Bible. Scriptural allusions proliferate throughout the novel: Liesel Driediger's "fall" (ch. 5) as she crosses a line which is at one and the same time the Equator, the boundary between girlhood and womanhood, and the distinction between innocence and experience; Anna

Friesen's meeting with Joseph Hiebert at the well (ch. 7), reminiscent of a similar meeting between Rachel and Jacob in the twenty-ninth chapter of Genesis; Samuel Reimer's being called by God (ch. 12) like his namesake in the Old Testament; the gathering around John Reimer's cross, which is Christ's (ch. 13). By the end, the challenge of new ideas and responses is specifically linked with the relation of the New Testament to the Old (see, in particular, Reimer's observations on the last page). Like the Bible, *The Blue Mountains of China* is a story of individual men that develops into a vast symbolic story of the human race. In this novel, more unequivocally than in *Peace Shall Destroy Many*, the Mennonites are presented not just as an individual people but as representatives of the aspirations and failures of all mankind.

In comparison with the scope and challenge of the earlier novels, Wiebe's canvas here is vast. We can trace, indeed, a consistent broadening of horizons. *Peace Shall Destroy Many* is deliberately limited to the small Mennonite community of Wapiti. Except for the flashback to Deacon Block's experiences in Russia, and the accounts of army life and the Second World War that Thom Wiens hears through the radio, Joseph Dueck's letter, and Hank Unger's bragging anecdotes, we stay within the narrow confines of the settlement. *First and Vital Candle* probes further. Though centred on Frozen Lake, it opens in Winnipeg, and the sections in which Abe Ross relives incidents in his past take us to the Arctic, to continental Europe during the Second World War, and to his prairie childhood. But *The Blue Mountains of China* ranges from Russia to Paraguay to China to Canada. While the earlier novels centred upon a single protagonist and a limited cast of characters, this one contains so many participants, and the relations between them are so complex and important, that the list of "Principal Characters in This Book" is a welcome and necessary aid at the beginning of the novel.

Wiebe has a complicated story to tell, but the opening sentences of the book establish an impression of perfected control:

I have lived long. So long, it takes me days to remember even parts of it, and some I can't remember at all until I've been thinking over it a little now and then for weeks, and little Johann or Friedl ask, "Urgrossmuttchi, what is that, so cold in Canada the ground is stiff?" Then I have to be careful or I'll start making it up, they like to hear so much. What I tell I remember only through God's grace. I never wrote anything down and didn't have more than the usual Mennonite village school, four or five years between fall and spring work. Then that was very good in Manitoba, if you got it, though it isn't anything at all there now. Or even here. But the Lord led me through so many deep ways and of the world I've seen a little, both north and south. If your eyes stay open and He keeps your head clear you sometimes see so much more than you want of how it is with the world. And if you don't you can thank Him for that, too. (7)

Part of the immediacy of this is explained, of course, by the abrupt plunge into first-person reminiscence. But there is an extra-ordinary authority about it as well. We must read it not only for its content but for the tone of the human voice that comes to us through the rhythms and phrasing. Frieda Friesen, we come to realize, is both maturely placid and irrepressibly garrulous; her speech combines the dignified and the colloquial. Before she tells us of her limited Mennonite schooling, we have become aware of a foreign accent, not merely through the use of "Urgrossmuttchi" but through syntax and emphasis ("what is that, so cold in Canada the ground is stiff?"). Yet this is, in its own way, an eloquent prose; it expresses, directly and economically, the sincerity and openness of the speaker.

Of all the voices that go to make up *The Blue Mountains of China*, Frieda Friesen's is the most straightforward and the most reliable. It is essential for Wiebe to establish our confidence in his initial narrator because his first challenge in approaching his ambitious scheme is to solve some pressing problems of construction. As I have already indicated, the scheme involves juxtaposing incidents occurring at different times to different people in different parts of the world. Wiebe has to avoid the danger of individual chapters lapsing into separate, unintegrated short stories. The fact that several of the sections ("Black Vulture," "Over the Red Line," "The Well," even Frieda's memoir) had been previously published on their own and had proved self-sufficient indicates the extent of the danger. But Wiebe overcomes the difficulty in several ways, the recurrent use of Frieda being one of the most important. The complete novel is divided into thirteen chapters, no less than four of them being told by Frieda under the continuing heading, "My Life: That's As It Was." These sections tell a straightforward chronicle-story from her birth in Manitoba in 1883 through her marriage and the departure with her growing family to a new life in Paraguay; it extends, indeed, through her long lifetime to include a return visit to Canada after her husband's death in 1958. The account is representative, almost documentary. By contrast, the other sections offer significant moments—some of them gripping and climactic like "Black Vulture" and "Drink Ye All of It" where groups of Mennonites face political oppression in Russia, others symbolic and epiphanic like "Over the Red Line" and "The Well" where individuals are involved in scenes of personal crisis. All reveal essential aspects of the Mennonite quest.

As a member of the Sommerfelder branch of Mennonites, Frieda represents one of the more conservative groups with emphasis on strict adherence to traditional Mennonite ways. But in her this conservatism has not become stultified or oppressive; there is none of the sourness, even rottenness, that we detect in Deacon Block's Wapiti. Frieda's is a way of life that, despite the harrowing journey to Paraguay, is basically quiet and uneventful, and the touching simplicity of her faith, her unshakeable conviction derived from her father that "it does come all from God, strength and sickness, want and plenty" (10, etc.), can exist side by side with an endearing humour. This humour needs to be insisted upon because it can easily elude the non-Mennonite reader. Wiebe has himself described its effect on those accustomed to the subtleties of intonation and gesture: "In *The Blue Moun-*

tains of China I tried to capture both the contorted language and self-deprecating humour of prairie Mennonites in a woman named Frieda Friesen. Once . . . I read parts of Frieda's monologue to several hundred Canadian Mennonites and they laughed themselves silly" (*VL*, 209). Outsiders can probably never respond in quite this way, but they can at least acknowledge the richness and, in essentials, the completeness of Frieda's life. They should also be able to recognize the way in which she acts as a yardstick for the rest of the Mennonite story.

Wiebe employs two basic methods for binding his material together, and the first depends on Frieda. Her sections are distributed carefully through the narrative—with mathematical precision, indeed—in chapters 1, 3, 6, and 10. They are thus interspersed with one, two, and three chapters respectively. We enter the story, gently, through her initial account, and this is juxtaposed with "Sons and Heirs," the story of Jakob Friesen V, a remote relative. The contrast, involving Wiebe's counterpointing of peace with violence, is extreme but Wiebe is able to move confidently, without any sense of strain, from Canada to Russia, from a characteristically female viewpoint to an indisputably male reaction, from the time-numbed memories of the old to the bitter and doomed present of the young. Then, so that as readers we may retain our bearings, we return to Frieda's story. After that, two new sets of characters are introduced before we hear Frieda's voice again, and then three before her final appearance. The ramifications of these later sections need not be discussed at this point; it is sufficient to note that Wiebe places her accounts structurally within the novel in order that we may have a constant point of reference. Similarly, on the moral level, Frieda represents a normative position against which others may be measured.

The second device, though possibly more conspicuous, is ultimately more subtle. Although the majority of the chapters are devoted to the fortunes of separate groups, two of them, placed strategically in both the design and the timespan of the novel, may be called "points of intersection." These are the fourth chapter, "Black Vulture," relating events that took place in Russia in 1929, and the final chapter, "On the Way," set at the side of an Alberta highway in 1967. In these chapters, representatives of all the main Mennonite families that appear in the novel come together. In the first, Friesens, Epps and Balzers (=Reimers) share a lodging-house in Moscow, and Helmut Driediger is active off-stage; their lives and fates intertwine at a significant moment in space and time. In the second, Jakob Friesen IV, John Reimer, Elizabeth Driediger, and the Will[ia]ms family converge "on the way" a generation later, with the Epps mentioned off-stage. The saga is thus appropriately rounded off.

These two scenes are of particular significance because they bring us close to the heart of the novel. Together they embody an important theme that Wiebe has touched on in his earlier novels but makes the keystone of this one: the possibly life-transforming influence of one person upon another. This sounds tame enough when set down baldly, but the implications are crucial to the Christianity of Wiebe and the Mennonites. The individual life can and, ideally, should be an example. In *Peace Shall Destroy Many*, Thom is helped by the example of Joseph Dueck ("his friendship with Thom had unlocked new thought possibilities of which Thom had formerly had no conception" [*PDM*, 17]) and tries in turn to pass on an example to those he teaches. The point is made more strongly in *First and Vital Candle*, where God seems to work through Sally Howell ("all that she had been and promised to be was flickering, alive in him" [*FVC*, 354]). Here, in *The Blue Mountains of China*, the effect is both less direct and more complex. After Jakob Friesen IV has been taken away by the Russians in "Black Vulture," Balzer/Reimer selfishly praises God for the sparing of his own family and is rebuked by David Epp: "Ernst, I think Mrs. Friesen was praying too" (66). That remark, spoken in Moscow in 1929 and apparently questioning God's concern for the individual life, bears fruit forty years later in Manitoba. It is a moment recalled by Balzer's son, Samuel U. Reimer, and plays its part in driving him towards his noble if quixotic mission to proclaim peace in Vietnam (see 127, 223, 225). Similarly, David Epp II makes an apparently pointless sacrifice on the Russo-Chinese border a year after the scene in Moscow. Although his family and the rest of their community have escaped across the frontier, he returns voluntarily to Russia to take the responsibility upon himself in the forlorn hope that he may possibly save others from suffering under reprisals. Itself a contrast with Balzer/Reimer's selfishness, as R.P. Bilan has pointed out,[2] it becomes an inspiration to his son David Epp III that determines his whole life. Samuel Reimer explains: "This David Epp never saw his father. . . . But he's made his whole life around what he knows his father did" (172). Even if the action had no influence in Russia in 1930, its consequences were to be seen in Paraguay in the 1960s. The whole system of interconnections that Wiebe records in this novel needs to be seen not in terms of novelistic coincidence but as an illustration of the principle that "No man is an Island." Here once again the Mennonites are presented as "symbols" for mankind as a whole.

But if *The Blue Mountains of China* bears witness to the possible potency of human example, it certainly doesn't neglect or ignore the darker side of human experience. For a novel dealing with the frustrating history of the Mennonites (who never reach their symbolic blue mountains), such a situation would be unthinkable. Those like Frieda Friesen who maintain the traditional standards are outnumbered by others who lose not only their faith but any sense of a meaning in life. Wiebe recreates the conditions endured by Mennonites in Russia and in their flights from Russia (the louse-infected hovels and starvation-diet in China, for instance) and the precarious nature of human life in Paraguay (in "Wash, This Sand and Ashes," David Epp III forces John Reimer to face the reality of "an Ayerooa with one leg" [153³].) Samuel U. Reimer's crusade is doomed from the start not only by the Canadian state but by the Mennonite church, and his awakening from materialist lethargy is misunderstood and betrayed by his own family; the possibility that his example of sacrifice may ultimately have an effect on his TV-degraded children is left open, but it seems remote. Wiebe clearly has no illusions about the world in which he and his characters find themselves.

But the nadir of human existence is reached, of course, by Jakob Friesen IV in "The Cloister of the Lilies." The man arrested by the Russians at the end of the fourth chapter now emerges, four chapters and several years later, in Siberia. An abandoned monastery where Christians had come "far away so no one could find them" (107)—one thinks of the Wapiti community in *Peace Shall Destroy Many*—ironically becomes the setting for the most chilling presentation of human evil. Jakob's deadened existence is roused into awareness by the nameless fugitive who allows his equally nameless and dying wife to be sexually assaulted by the Russian soldiers ("To them she is a hole" [113]) in the hope that they will allow the couple to escape. The man combines the relics of a faith ("There is the possibility, as God is good" [113]) with a tough grass-roots philosophy of life ("There is only this: if you want anything, survive. There is nothing else" [113]). In the darkness, he utters the sentence that becomes for Jakob a teasingly ambiguous statement of what has become known (too glibly) as "the human condition":

> "To live, it is the most necessary possibility."
>
> Friesen was never sure to what question the man gave this answer. Whenever he thought about what they had whispered in that nameless ruin, he and the faceless immobile man whose name and place he never knew, before whose immobile suffering his own had finally broken between his teeth, sometimes he thought the man meant that to live was the essential; sometimes that to live a good God was the essential; sometimes that to live, to survive and to suffer was the essential; sometimes that any one of them could be the most essential. Any one a possibility. And sometimes the possibility was all of these things essential at the same time, any one impossible without any one other, and after one spasm of thought it did not mean any of them at all. Whatever the man had said had been some kind of stupidity, some punch-deadened prisoner's immovable madness that sometimes, just as thought touched it, seemed for an instant

to blaze with a kind of holy wisdom that was[,] that could be known, but never said. If he remembered it correctly; later he could never be quite sure about that either. (114-5)

This is, I am convinced, a central passage, and noteworthy as an example of Wiebe's raising issues within the narrative that might in his earlier work have appeared in too baldly didactic a form. Here, however, we are conscious of Friesen's dilemma, not the ideas of a moralizing author. The man's words haunt Friesen. In the final section, we sense that his tight-lipped profession of atheism ("I believe nothing" [193, 196, 222]) masks a deeply personal if unformulated faith. "To live, it is the most necessary possibility": the first and vital candle burns on, albeit weakly, in Jakob Friesen IV, and the nameless man's enigmatic statement is at least partly responsible. Like David Epp I's rebuke to Balzer and David Epp II's return to Russia, this sentence also serves as an example—and has consequences. Its ambiguity is matched by the uncertainty of Jakob's response: is it his faith that has "finally broken between his teeth" or, as the syntax would suggest, his suffering? If it contains faith, it is a faith reduced to the lowest common factor of its components. But "possibility" is a word that recurs with effect throughout this section, and, like the lilies on the cloister wall, Christian symbols emerging "in sudden pure white" from beneath the grime (106), the possibility of faith remains available under the surface of life.

But a related point also needs to be made. In "The Cloister of the Lilies" Wiebe manages to present human corruption without grovelling in his subject-matter. He does not (like those Mennonites who withdrew to Wapiti or Paraguay) turn his back on the depths of human behaviour in the hope of escaping its taint. Thus he faithfully reproduces the obscenities of the Russian soldiers, but the effect achieved is the reverse of obscene. This is one of the qualities, I believe, that set his work apart from so much contemporary writing. At this point degradation is his subject, but the people he presents are not themselves degraded (at least, not the Mennonites—the Russian guards degrade themselves).

Men are resolutely judged according to a moral standard, a standard that the novel itself reflects at all times. It is not coincidental that, in the last chapter, we find the following sentiments put into the thoughts of Elizabeth Driediger:

> She wanted to groan in pain for what she understood of [Jakob Friesen], of herself, and at the same time rage flared in her at the guilt and agony and regret covering, soaked through and through people while the "great" poets and novelists of the western world mucked around wading and parading their own mighty organs and viscera, posturing like puppets, shooting themselves off at the moon and inflating themselves the magnificent modern crusaders of humanity, seers and prophets of the sixties, because they "discovered" Stalin and Hitler, because they "discovered" Dachau, "discovered" Vietnam. Dachaus are everywhere; who could number the Vietnams. In people who believe they believe nothing. (196-7)

The ideas are consonant, one feels, with Wiebe's own position,[4] but once again they have been integrated into the texture of the novel. And they echo Jakob Friesen himself, with his atheistic assertion which Elizabeth Driediger knows to be a lie. Friesen is an extremely complex figure; he is treated sympathetically within the novel—his suffering, his very survival, enforce our profound respect—but his role of "kulak" in post-1917 Russia and the circumstances surrounding his separation from his son do not pass without implicit criticism. Within the moral hierarchy that the novel insists upon, he does not attain the stature and authority of David Epp II or John Reimer.

We have come a long way from the straightforward chronicle of Frieda Friesen, and this in itself gives some indication of the extraordinary variety which Wiebe is able to contain within his novel. But this variety is not achieved without cost. Although, as I have suggested, Wiebe himself moves confidently and impressively between scene and scene, the beginning reader may well find the abrupt changes of setting and mood both confusing and frustrating. To take a convenient though not extreme example, the contrasts between chapters one and two, Frieda's first narrative and Jakob Friesen V's story, are particularly emphatic. "Sons and Heirs" opens in a Russian prison; as Ina Ferris has written, the "setting switches from the expanse of prairie to the confinement of a dark cell" (*VL*, 90). This second chapter presents a world beyond Frieda's powers of comprehension and also outside the experience of most readers. Violence replaces peace, the physical hardships of a shared community life are juxtaposed with the overpowering solitude of an isolated individual, and the only apparent point of connection is the surname, Jakob's father being a remote relative of Frieda. Moreover, Frieda's simplicity and engaging directness give way to the tortured and fragmented syntax of the young Jakob's stream of consciousness as he gropes confusedly in a world suddenly deprived of meaning and standards. The life of quotidian reality is replaced by a personal nightmare of crisis. The blurred, dark uncertainties of Jakob's story reflect the collapse of his Mennonite values, and as Jakob descends to the moral level of Escha, the Russian who had once been his servant (a deft correspondence to the material egalitarianism enforced by the communist regime), Wiebe insists that we follow Jakob into this shadow-world of temptation, violence, and lust.

Here we encounter the first conspicuous example of a recurring artistic problem in Wiebe's mature work. He knows that, if his ultimate effect is to be achieved, the reader must be forced to experience something comparable to the anguish of his characters. There is no place for emotional detachment in this kind of fiction. Whether Jakob is confronted by the methods and practices of the GPU (the Soviet secret service) or Big Bear is plunged into a bewildering white world, the reader must share the sense of disorientation, endure the shattering of hitherto unchallenged convictions and attitudes, know how it feels to tumble without hope into a physical or moral abyss. But the literary effects required to achieve all this—dislocation of expected syntax, puzzling time-shifts ("he lost grip on duration, on sequence," we are told of the imprisoned Jakob [12]), abrupt switches from external to internal viewpoint, disconcerting juxtapositions of incident and tone—all these threaten to alienate the reader. In striving for epic fiction, Wiebe takes considerable risks.

Here, for example, is one of the climactic scenes in "Sons and Heirs":

> He took the stall shovel, clotted and heavy, and silently found his place. The barn stood empty. At last the housedoor scraped and the other came, knuckles to his eyes, stretching, and striding up the aisle whistling. Strange; to sing so well yet whistle slightly off-key
>
> *blessed savior make   blessed savior make me hiieyah there hiieyahhh   pffft   like paper in fire get outta there there into the stall   get outta there slide in there where you belong   whoa now easy and tight you slippery devil   like fire blessed savior o my blessed savior make me*
>
> and he climbed the ladder. The girl sat erect into the sunlight coming through the doors, the smell as the first time, and said, "Oh." He stared down into her moist red mouth. She smiled a little, her dark mane swinging easily back and forth. In a lunge he kicked her red boots aside and fell on her softness and her sudden ringing laugh gurgled, snapped. (39-40)

The reader can be forgiven, I think, if he initially fails to realize that, in the pause in external action represented by the italicized interior monologue, Jakob kills Escha ("the other") with the shovel. On the other hand, when he does understand what has occurred, the resultant shock is an apt response to Jakob's defiance of the basic Mennonite principles of peace and sexual restraint.

We can appreciate in the scene as a whole an impressive buildup of emotional tension, appropriately taking the form of violence followed by sexual aggression and release; certainly, the overall effect of murky uncertainty is not without its force. Yet, even if we grant that a polished smoothness of style would be appallingly out of place in this context, the prevailing suspicion of vagueness and perhaps unnecessary difficulty remains. Where can a line be drawn between justified and unjustified obscurity? And this is by no means an isolated example; others, indeed, are far more problematic. Personal inquiry has revealed the fact that many sympathetic and intelligent readers find themselves asking basic questions about the details of the narrative: what precisely is Franz Epp's experience in the street near the Kremlin (69)? what exactly happens to Liesel Driediger when she falls through the rails of the ship (84)? what is the nature of the critical emergency that overtakes the Will[ia]ms family in the last chapter (217)? Properly, one feels, such questions should not need to be raised. Ultimately, perhaps, these details do not matter, but if the reader in the process of reading suspects that they could be crucial, his response to the novel as a whole may be seriously interrupted.

I have no confident or clear-cut answers to these questions. I believe that the difficulties are genuine, though I also believe that (like the notorious clumsinesses in the work of Frederick Philip Grove) they are minor irritants that need not seriously detract from the effectiveness of the whole. It has been said of Thomas Hardy that "he writes clumsily, but he writes creatively,"[5] and much the same might be said of Wiebe. Although we may regret the occasional smudges that threaten to obscure the clear lines of his work, we should also grant that the resultant roughness of texture is part of its strength and solidity. The reader must be prepared to trust Wiebe, to accept that the difficulties encountered in approaching his fiction are not without a purpose. There is no other Canadian novelist, I suspect, whose work more clearly demands, and deserves, re-reading.

Moreover, despite these obscurities of expression, Wiebe's range and variety is ultimately achieved in the only way in which it can properly be achieved, by means of language. I must insist upon the importance of language here because it is an essential ingredient of Wiebe's art and one that is most likely, I think, to be overlooked. It makes possible the remarkable control of tone that distinguishes the novel as a whole. Examples could be drawn from any chapter. Consider, for instance, the youthful exuberance of the young Elizabeth Driediger on shipboard in "Over the Red Line," a scene which, besides fulfilling its own place in the total design, provides a welcome relief from the harrowing tension of the earlier episodes; or the delicate idyllicism of "The Well" in which Frieda's daughter, enjoying "a quietness she knew as joy" (104), recalls the tempting possibility of a life outside the Mennonite restrictions that might have robbed her of the tranquillity and content that are, for her, fulfilment. (Despite the tonal differences, the thematic link between these two episodes—Liesel, in D.W. Doerksen's words, "flees *into* the world"[6] while Anna quietly rejects its temptations—constitutes an additional and characteristic effect.) But Wiebe's mastery of tone is especially noticeable in the last two chapters, and I want to concentrate on these since, on account of the episodic nature of the whole, the novel is either made or broken—and it is, surely, triumphantly made—by the success of the closing sections.

The penultimate chapter, "The Vietnam Call of Samuel U. Reimer," seems to me a masterpiece. The war in Vietnam, now fading into the junkyard of the embarrassing past (where are the fiascos of yesteryear?) provoked in its time so much feverish, emotionally indulgent writing that Wiebe's indirect, ironic, elusive but none the less cogent and committed approach is particularly welcome. Who else, one wonders, could create out of this material an episode so amusing, so touching, and above all so human as Reimer's pathetically unsuccessful effort to obey his ludicrous but sublime injunction? His Christian name draws attention to the biblical parallel-cum-parody (I Samuel 3) which succeeds in being humorous and serious at the same time, but its transplanting into the world and idiom of bourgeois Manitoba ("Shrunken meatloaf, carton of Slim-it milk, split celery; not one stupid thing in the whole stupid fridge" [158]) demands the total control and delicacy of touch that are the hallmarks of a truly

creative novelist. Thom Wiens's dilemma, his difficulty in understanding the relation between peace and violence, his realization
of the abyss between Mennonite (=Christian=human) theory and
Mennonite (=Christian=human) practice, is replayed in a different key, and the superficial comedy makes the resultant effect all
the more poignant. Simultaneously with our appreciation, at a
practical common-sense level, of the absurdity of the enterprise
comes a startling realization of the radical profundity of the
questions that Wiebe poses. What relation do we achieve between
the religious values to which many of us pay a cautious lip-service
and the actions (with all their attendant consequences) of our day-
to-day lives? To what extent are we responsible for the state of the
world in which we live? In a mad or evil world, who can recognize
sanity or godliness? These are questions that recur in varying
forms in Wiebe's novels—the sanity of Riel and his "visions" as
presented in *The Scorched-Wood People* are disturbingly similar
in their implications—but nowhere are they explored more
masterfully than here.

But it is the final chapter, "On the Way," that stretches
Wiebe's creative gifts to their fullest extent. At this point in the
novel, the thoughtful reader may well ask: how is it possible to
unify the heterogeneous material so far presented? how can the
numerous strands unloosed in the earlier stages of the narrative be
gathered together? But the strange evening rendezvous at the side
of a busy Alberta highway provides a hauntingly satisfying if
unexpected conclusion, and this is achieved, to a considerable
extent, by the careful blending of voices. The spectrum is broad.
At one extreme, we find the empty clichés of the motorcyclist who
offers gratuitous advice to the cross-carrying John Reimer, and
the debased speech of Irene Will[ia]ms who unwittingly demon-
strates the price in cultural continuity paid for material success
and who shows herself incapable of comprehending the extent of
her deprivation. The linguistic shock here is harsh—there are
readers who find it uncomfortably close to crude parody—but
Wiebe is challenging us to reconsider our attitudes to current
speech-patterns and their implications for cultural health, and

his examples (though admittedly condensed) may be less exagger-
ated than some will want to admit. Certainly, they represent the
lowest part of the scale that runs through the businessman's
jargon of Irene's father and the linguistically informed but
colloquially deadened speech of Elizabeth Driediger (whose
cynical but skin-deep university sophistication is skilfully
caught) to the tentative but sincere and so impressive talk of John
Reimer and—ironically, most eloquent of all—to the generally
silent presence of Jakob Friesen IV. Old and young, rich and poor,
Canadian and foreign, even (one reason for the presence of the
motorcyclist) Mennonite and non-Mennonite, converge together,
and we realize that the point of intersection recorded here
encompasses not only a representative group of the Mennonites of
1967 but (as the centenary date suggests) a microcosm of Canadian
society, and even of the contemporary world as a whole. The
surviving victim of totalitarian atrocity (that the totalitarianism
in question should be Communist rather than Fascist is itself a
reminder that Wiebe writes from a perspective maturely outside
the sentimental-leftist assumptions of the currently fashionable
literary "élite") stands side by side with the products of post-war
commercial prosperity and two kinds of youthful radicalism—the
one (John Reimer's) sober and considered, the other (the motorcyclist's) vacuous and irresponsible. Yet all these are not "types"
artificially conceived and patterned; each exists in his own right,
unique and incomparable.

I have already indicated that I consider "On the Way" a
remarkably successful concluding chapter. Recently, however,
more critical assessments of this section have appeared in print.
Ina Ferris complains that "exploration gives way to assertion"
here and that John Reimer (who must, she thinks, be "a compelling presence") "emerges as a rational, imposed and self-
conscious symbol, relying heavily—and inappropriately—on
statement" (*VL*, 94, 95). My own more positive view is linked with
my conviction that John Reimer's position is not offered as an
answer but only as a tentative groping in what appears to be the
right direction. There can, of course, be no neat resolution

because that would be untrue to the precarious human situation in the second half of the twentieth century. An "open ending" is clearly required. On the other hand, all is not gloom; the human interconnections between the Mennonites and ex-Mennonites who meet around John Reimer's enigmatic cross are fragile, but they still exist. That Jakob Friesen's words "resonate as John Reimer's fail to do" (*VL*, 95) is, I think, part of the point: an acknowledgment of the difficulty of Christian witness. The most overtly didactic statements in the whole novel certainly occur in this last chapter, and, as we might expect, they are put into the mouth of John Reimer. But although his "message" has respectable and impressive Mennonite analogues (its argument is traced out at greater length and in more scholarly detail by John Howard Yoder, the Mennonite theologian, in *The Politics of Jesus* [1972], a book about which Wiebe has spoken in praise [*VL*, 243]), it needs to be considered, and scrutinized, within its fictional context. Like some of the conversations involving Rupert Birkin in D.H. Lawrence's *Women in Love,* the sentiments are tested by the circumstances under which they are spoken. Ultimately, the meaning of this concluding chapter resides in the totality of experience that it encompasses. All the characters (not to mention the author and his readers) are "on the way," and Reimer's cross-carrying is an act open to numerous interpretations ranging from a literal and moving imitation of Christ to an incongruous gesture out of touch with modern realities. Neither Reimer nor his creator is likely to view his meditations as in any sense fixed or absolute. No moralizing preacher, and certainly no "compelling presence," Reimer offers himself as "just a tired, dying human being, walking the land" (225); this self-description is, in itself, an index to his maturity and to his (inevitable) limitation.

Those who see Wiebe's "message" as contained in Reimer's sermon (ironically interrupted, we notice, by a courteous but firm policeman [215-6]) forget that the novel has a further ten pages to go. Wiebe's position, I would argue, is more complex and can be found embodied in the final inconclusive discussion between Reimer and Friesen. The balancing implied by their association at this point is profoundly appropriate. Reimer, needless to say, is not offered as in any sense a Christ figure, yet his ideal has the same combination of sublime simplicity and practical difficulty that we find in Christ's teachings. Jakob Friesen is understandably doubtful, but his quietly phrased statement of discipleship, "I want to walk with him" (216), should not pass unnoticed. In these two the elaborate threads that have been established in earlier sections—threads involving faith and unfaith, peace and violence, conservatism and new ideas—come into at least a temporary relation. Thus their final discussion in the twilight echoes gently but palpably the scene between Friesen and the unnamed fugitive in "The Cloister of the Lilies":

> "If you had been ten years in exile and survived and then dragged yourself back fifteen years and found everything wiped clean like cheap plastic, you would say nothing."
>
> "I have never known that, so I cannot say. But," a wind moved high in the trees, "surely even then I could know, as I know now, that as long as I am alive the possibility can never be completely closed that God is good."
>
> "Ah-h-h. If there is one."
>
> "That possibility cannot be closed, either." (225-6)

This statement of the impossibility of closure can also be applied to Wiebe's novel. While the numerous thematic strands in the novel may not be fully disentangled, at least they can be seen as expertly drawn together.

The novel ends, aptly, on a muted note. As R.P. Bilan has written, "Jakob is sceptical to the end, but John [Reimer] has the last word."[7] The "blue mountains" emblematic of the Mennonite—and human—quest are visible at the horizon but the real object of the quest (in Reimer's words) "isn't anywhere on earth" (227). We begin to realize that the blue mountains can be profoundly ambiguous in meaning, that they can represent, in the words of one commentator, "the mistakenly idealistic withdrawal from the 'world'—that is, from Christian involvement with other people."[8] Yet the novel leaves us not on a note of stalemate but with a sense of enlargement comparable to that paradoxical feeling of exultation we experience at the close of a tragedy. Ultimately, the effectiveness of the ending depends not so much on the acceptability of Reimer's "message" or even on the combination of Mennonite qualities represented by Reimer and Jakob Friesen IV but on Wiebe's success in embodying, within the novel as a whole, the physical and spiritual history of a people.[9] *The Blue Mountains of China*, indeed, justifies Wiebe's impressive generalization about the capacity of the novel as an art-form: "I think fiction is one of the great ways one can express one's hopes and aspirations . . . for what humanity is capable of."[10]

5 The Temptations of Big Bear

At the end of *The Blue Mountains of China*, John Reimer decides to continue his journey not west into the mountains, emblems of an attractive but elusive "promised land," but north. As he explains to Jakob Friesen IV, "after Edmonton and a few towns there are only Indian reserves, Métis cabins, and a few Mennonite settlements, and then nothing but the land" (*BMC*, 227). This decision to change direction was Wiebe's also. His creative work in the 1970s has followed an analogous pattern; eschewing the idealistic quest for a future paradise on earth beyond the next blue mountains, he delves into the past of the Canadian land, into the culture of the Indians and the Métis, not to avoid the present but in order to understand it.

Though the role of Louis Riel and the Métis in the prairie disturbances of 1885 is well known, that of Big Bear and the Indians (which Wiebe chose to explore first) is decidedly less familiar. Acknowledged as a powerful chief of the Plains Cree, Big Bear had had the foresight to mistrust the terms and conditions laid out in the Indian treaties, and for some years he resolutely (the whites claimed, obstinately) refused either to sign a treaty or to accept a reservation. As the situation of the Indians deteriorated after the disappearance of the buffalo, he found himself increasingly isolated and unable to control the younger and more militant members of his band. Ultimately, the unrest erupted into violence at Frog Lake where, despite Big Bear's attempts to prevent bloodshed, nine whites were killed. Subsequently he was found responsible for the actions of his band and sentenced to three years' imprisonment by a white court. He died soon after his release.

Big Bear's story appealed to Wiebe for several reasons, not least because of its tragic and "epic" possibilities—the decline of the hero parallelling the decline of his people, the man of peace caught like his earlier protagonists in a web of violence, a noble individual destroyed by the inexorable clash of cultures. However, Wiebe first became attracted to Big Bear not so much for historical or artistic but for what might loosely be called sentimental motives, the fact that his own birthplace lay in the area in which Big Bear and the remnants of his band of Plains Cree had wandered half a century before. But the same accident of birth had also led him (less painfully, one suspects, than his own Thom Wiens) to accept Indians naturally as neighbours and fellow-citizens, not as aliens set apart on reservations. "I write about Indians," he told George Melnyk, "because I grew up in communities where they were part of the people" (*VL*, 205). Moreover, as a member of a minority ethnic group himself, he recognized the need, once he had explored the cultural history of his own people, to set the Indian in his rightful place within Canadian literature. This became, in the early 1970s, something resembling a cultural crusade for Wiebe. In an important essay on Western Canadian fiction, published in 1971, he wrote: "The Indian . . . must become our central, not our fringe figure, exotic, a bit mysterious perhaps, but mostly drunken and prostituted; he must become the center of serious fiction as other groups have."[1]

Once he began his investigations into the history of the Indians in the area in which he had been brought up, Wiebe found even more compelling reasons for interest in Big Bear: "I felt very strongly that here was an incredibly great man, who had never been talked about, almost totally unknown" (*VL*, 154).[2] Thus the possibility evolved, slowly but relentlessly, of making Big Bear the centre of a novel, and this immediately committed

Wiebe to an intensive bout of serious historical research. He had read William Bleasdell Cameron's personal reminiscences, *The War Trail of Big Bear*, in the late 1950s and William B. Fraser's pamphlet, *Big Bear: Indian Patriot*, a year or so after its publication in 1966 (see *VL*, 133), but there followed a detailed study of histories, newspapers, memoirs, archives, as well as meticulous investigations "in the field," including Indian reservations where he spoke with some of Big Bear's descendants.[3] He even went so far as to track down his "power-bundle" preserved in a New York Museum (see *VL*, 143-9). Wiebe has become, in short, a recognized authority on Big Bear and his tribe, and it is fitting that he should have been invited to write the life of the Plains Cree leader for the *Dictionary of Canadian Biography* (volume 11, scheduled for publication in 1981). He has recorded that, all in all, research for the novel took him four years, the writing an additional two (see *VL*, 166); moreover, after assimilating all this varied and often contradictory material, he still had to face complicated artistic and philosophical questions concerning the relation of history to fiction. Since these matters are essential for an appreciation of the artistry of *The Scorched-Wood People* as well as for *The Temptations of Big Bear*, they deserve to be considered in some detail.

The problem was not, of course, altogether new to Wiebe. Although the characters in *The Blue Mountains of China* were imaginary, they were caught up in moments of history that had to be presented accurately and with a sense of tonal authenticity. The life of the *Kanadier* Mennonites in Manitoba at the close of the last century, the precarious situation of those attempting to leave Russia in the late 1920s, the conditions in the new communities in the "green hell" of Paraguay (*BMC*, 48): all these had to conform to at least the basic standards of historical and sociological reliability. (Wiebe had created many of the sections in this novel out of the reminiscences of older Mennonite neighbours,[4] and he has stated that he would never have been able to write the Paraguay scenes before he had personally visited the Mennonite settlements there [see *VL*, 239]). Frieda Friesen's chapter-titles, "My Life: That's As It Was," imply a representational truth with respect to historical as well as personal experience. But in *The Temptations of Big Bear* the problem is magnified since, as Wiebe is justifiably proud to point out, "every single person that appears in the novel is an historical person."[5]

In his historical romances, Sir Walter Scott had placed fictional characters like Waverley and Francis Osbaldistone side by side with historical figures like Bonnie Prince Charlie and Rob Roy in real places at precise moments in historical time; similarly, in an instance Wiebe has himself discussed (*VL*, 217), Tolstoy has the imaginary Pierre walking across an actual battlefield and coming into contact with historical figures including Napoleon and Kutuzov. The practice had become a convention, though it had not escaped critical censure. On the publication of *Waverley* in 1814, John Wilson Croker had complained in the *Quarterly Review* that "we have a great objection . . . to historical romance, in which real and fictitious personages and actual and fabulous events are mixed together to the utter confusion of the reader and the unsettling of all accurate recollections of past transaction."[6] Wiebe's decision to limit himself to documented characters answers Croker's particular complaint but proves itself even more vulnerable to his more generalized sense of unease. Croker would have preferred Scott to write a history of the Jacobite uprising rather than a "romance"; if Wiebe sticks to "historical persons," why write a novel instead of a history of Frog Lake and the rebellion of 1885? The question is not as naive as its bald statement may suggest, and Wiebe clearly took it seriously. "The thing I'm tussling with in this new book," he told Donald Cameron in 1971, "is how you present facts."[7] This in turn raises various (and subtler) questions: what is the distinction between fact and fiction? in what respects does Wiebe's method of reconstruction differ from that of a professional historian? can a valid distinction be maintained between the imaginative and the imaginary? to what extent can Wiebe's work be judged by historical as distinct from aesthetic criteria?

"The problem is how to make the story" (*WV*, 135). This is the opening sentence of the short story "Where is the Voice

Coming From?", written in 1970 and first published in 1971—at precisely the time when Wiebe was beginning the actual writing of *The Temptations of Big Bear*. Wiebe's emphasis throughout his career has been on the craft of making; we should remember that one of his anthologies of short fiction is entitled not, as we might expect, *The Story-Tellers* but *The Story-Makers*. The same point is made in a recent article. All forms of fiction, he insists, "are things made (Latin *fictio*, a shaping, a feigning), in contrast to things done (Latin *factum*, something done, a deed)" (*VL*, 217). In "Where is the Voice Coming From?" the story-making persona finds the traditional distinctions between "history" and "story" inadequate. He quotes Teilhard de Chardin ("We are continually inclined to isolate ourselves from the things and events which surround us . . . as though we were spectators, not elements in what goes on" [*WV*, 135]) and Aristotle ("The true difference [between the historian and the poet] is that one relates what *has* happened, the other what *may* happen" [*WV*, 141]). He then comments:

> these statements cannot explain the story-teller's activity since, despite the most rigid application of impersonal investigation, the elements of the story have now run me underground. If ever I could, I can no longer pretend to objective, omnipotent disinterestedness. . . . I am no longer *spectator* of what *has* happened or what *may* happen: I am become *element* in what is happening at this very moment. (*WV*, 141-2)

This brings us at least a little closer to a viable distinction. Much as he is fascinated by facts, perhaps as a result of his Mennonite upbringing and its suspicion of created "lies," Wiebe knows that the fictional "maker" cannot limit himself to facts. As he remarked to Eli Mandel, "the fact is always in the past, but a fiction is what you make of it" (*VL*, 152). Even the historian can never avoid interpretation completely (since any kind of selection of documentary evidence, any emphasis on one aspect of an event rather than another, involves interpretation of some sort, an injection of judgment on to the "raw" fact); but the artist unabashedly thrives on it. His creative faculty is manifest in the convincing motivation he provides (*i.e.* invents) for his protagonist and the artistic balance that he achieves—"artfully," as we say—in his selection and moulding of available incident. Moreover, objectivity may be an official virtue in a historian, but a novelist like Wiebe will find it less than sacrosanct. Once again, a statement from his interview with Mandel, while *The Temptations of Big Bear* was being discussed, is pertinent: "The book is my way of looking at the world, and that's why I called it a novel and I don't pretend that it's a history which is written impartially. It's written in a very biased way" (*VL*, 152).

The presumed impartiality of the historian need not be challenged at this point, though we shall need to return to the matter when considering *The Scorched-Wood People*. In *The Temptations of Big Bear*, Wiebe relies upon, and often reproduces, the documents that provide the raw materials for the historian, and he too must not only select and interpret them but also adjudicate between them when, as he notes with pleasure, they contradict themselves (see *VL*, 138). For Wiebe, however, the official records tell only one side of the story—they are invariably white records compiled for white purposes and intended for white readers. The interpretation of Big Bear that is built up in this way contrasts dramatically with the sympathetic impression that we derive from the novel as a whole. The effect that Wiebe describes in *The Story-Makers* as "*camera-eye internal*,"[8] already employed in the presentation of Jakob Friesen V and David Epp II in *The Blue Mountains of China*, is also applied at key moments in *The Temptations of Big Bear* to the Indian chief. The Indian view and the various white views are therefore juxtaposed—often, indeed, set deliberately in conflict.

In order to gain this effect, Wiebe sometimes has to create appropriate documents. Occasionally, this is rendered unavoidable because of an unfortunate gap in the historical evidence. Big Bear's address to the court at the time of his sentencing, for example, does not survive in the Parliamentary records, and Wiebe had no alternative but to reconstruct it from William Bleasdell Cameron's summary (see *VL*, 138). But aesthetic considerations cause him to go further. Thus Kitty McLean's impression of Big Bear is needed in preference to that of her elder sisters because (like Hal Wiens in *Peace Shall Destroy Many*) she is young enough to see the Indian chief without the blinkers of convention that dictate the response of the older white prisoners. "Even Papa," she observes, "would never understand Big Bear's comprehension" (286). If her memoirs do not exist, they must needs be invented. At this point, of course, historian and novelist part company, but it would be a mistake to see the distinction as one between incomplete records and undisciplined invention; although the novelist's recreation can never be proven either accurate or inaccurate in all its details, it may well embrace an imaginative truth. For Wiebe, historical records can at best provide no more than a partial view; it is the artist's opportunity and privilege—even, perhaps, his moral responsibility—to augment them by plunging them once again into the rounded if contradictory complexity of life in the process of being lived.

The meticulous historical reconstruction demanded by *The Temptations of Big Bear,* though it can be seen as an extension of the method employed in *The Blue Mountains of China,* none the less involved Wiebe in so many intellectual and aesthetic problems that it can be legitimately hailed as a new departure. But his great theme here, as in all his earlier work, is the relation between human groups and the land upon which they live. In delving back into the nineteenth-century history of the north-west, he was probing a peculiarly Canadian version of this relation. The tone is set on the first page, where Alexander Morris, the lieutenant-governor of Manitoba at the time of the Fort Pitt treaty of September 1876, thinks about "the several hundred thousand square miles to which he had finally and forever extinguished, as the Prime Minister liked to say it, all native rights" (9). So much for the predominating white viewpoint; but the Indian attitude, we soon discover, is very different. In Big Bear's words: "No one can choose for only himself a piece of the Mother Earth. She is. And she is for all that live, alike. . . . Who can receive land? From whom would he receive it?'' (28, 29) Much later, Big Bear develops the point with equal force: "If we respect and honour the Queen because of her great work on the Earth, how much more must we honour the Earth? Is this queen more to us than the Earth? The proper way to live upon the Earth is to give each one the right the First One gave every one man. Let every man walk where his feet can walk" (199-200).

For Wiebe, then, the prairie unrest that came to a head at Frog Lake and Batoche is not so much a struggle for power between two opposed forces or even a moral conflict between right and wrong, justice and injustice. More fundamentally, it is a tragic (because unavoidable) clash between two irreconcilable ways of looking at human beings and their environment. Here again we see the characteristic interest of the artist rather than the historian. There are, naturally, elements of power-politics inherent in the whole episode, and these generate a confrontation with profound moral implications. But Wiebe lays his emphasis on the crucial underlying determinant, recognizable clearly. enough now but not generally comprehended a century ago: that the whites, however sincere or insincere they may have been, were incapable of appreciating the fact that the Indians looked at the land with totally different preconceptions from their own. Stated bluntly, and this helps to explain Wiebe's special interest in the matter, the white viewpoint was primarily commercial and economic (Schultz, in *The Scorched-Wood People*, significantly refers to "a land just waiting to be taken" [*SWP*, 92]), while that of the Indians was fundamentally religious.

This difference between white and Indian attitudes was, for Wiebe, both a problem and a challenge. The situation contains tensions that can provide stimulating fictional material, but, since he writes for a predominantly white audience, he must reproduce and embody within his prose an attitude that is, by the very nature of the subject, difficult for his readers to respond to. It is one thing to recognize the clash of cultural assumptions; it is altogether another to react with equal (or even greater) sympathy to the other side. Here was a problem far more complex than the serious presentation of Mennonite life in *Peace Shall Destroy Many* or even *The Blue Mountains of China*. Fortunately, however, Wiebe now possessed both the experience and the technical inventiveness to rise to the occasion. He was able to bring to bear all his resources of verbal power and constructional skill in order to make us appreciate the Indian response—not just comprehend it intellectually but feel it inwardly, on our pulses.

"Sweetgrass had signed the treaty" (9). The opening words not only set the action in a historical (and documented) past but create an effect of distanced irony since the reader, unlike some of the participants, knows only too well what the practical consequences of having signed the treaty will be. What he can deduce with the privilege of hindsight, however, Big Bear knows through "vision," a quality in which Sweetgrass himself is sadly deficient. But this opening scene, although the first sentence belongs to Sweetgrass, goes on to present the familiar white man's perspective. As I have already noted, the extinguishing of native land-rights is already a *fait accompli*. Moreover, the emphasis is laid, unostentatiously but unmistakably, on material issues: the possible breaking of pens by the Indians as they clumsily attach their X marks to the treaty, and the waste of time, in the lieutenant-governor's view, as the requisite ritual goes on. The first conversation, between governor Morris and the clerk John Kerr (whose earlier career was to be recounted by Wiebe in *The Scorched-Wood People*) concerns Kerr's performance in the Indian dance the night before when he had parodied the squaws in their presence. A subsequent discussion of Gabriel Dumont ("that Dumont" [12]) reveals a basic insensitivity to native desires and grievances: "The police are here now. Indians or halfbreeds, it makes no difference" (13). While it is true, as R.P. Bilan has observed, that in terms of plot very little happens in this first scene (*VL*, 172), the tensions and injustices that are later to be fanned into violence are firmly and often subtly established. The practical, workmanlike white position is reflected in a clear but unimaginative prose, the dialogue frequently lapsing into slang and cliché; power and bureaucratic organization prevail.

"My heart rises like a bird to see you once more" (17). Sweetgrass's opening speech in the second section is courtly, obsequious, and rather quaintly old-fashioned, but it alerts us to the power of words, to distinctions of voice that have not been evident hitherto. All this leads up, with growing anticipation on the part of the reader, to the first words of Big Bear: "I find it hard, to speak" (19). And a moment later: "There is a stone between me and what I have to say" (20). Throughout the book, Big Bear's speeches are marked by a diffident yet eloquent simplicity and a visionary, metaphoric quality that manages to combine mystery with lucidity. In his first extended speech, explaining his refusal to sign the treaty or be baptised into the white man's Christianity, he expresses the Indian religious oneness with the land in words whose rhythmic emphases are at least as effective as their meaning:

> ... I am fed by the Mother Earth. The only water I will be touched by comes from above, the rain from the Only One who makes the grass grow and the rivers run and the buffalo feed there and drink so that I and my children live. That we have life! (23)

The conflicting attitudes of white and Indian, expressed in argument and assertion, are also embodied in language, in distinctive modes of speech.

The third section reverts to a white viewpoint, in this case the story of the sympathetic missionary George McDougall, who faces death on the plains in Indian fashion—"he had found a level spot and properly laid himself out, limbs straight and hands folded up on his breast" (47)—and so prefigures Big Bear's journey to the Sand Hills at the end of the novel. His story is told by McDougall's son with a crisp narrative directness. Intent once again upon dramatic juxtaposition, Wiebe sets the fourth section in the Indian camp, bringing it vividly to life in passages of highly sensuous descriptive prose. Here is an instance:

> Into the coned warmth of the lodge, a thick weighed dark-
> ness of roasting meat and women and firelight and fur; soft
> darkness of leather and people sweat; darkness moving like
> raw yearling buffalo hung headless, turning in the complete
> circle of living and solid sweet immovable and ever changing
> Earth; darkness of fat's slip and dripping, of birch bark
> curling light, a darkness soft in flares of burning blood like
> the raw heat of women tunneled and spent for love. (51)

Here and throughout the novel, Wiebe contrasts the unified
sensibility of Indian living, the physical and spiritual in perfect
fusion, with the "fallen," bifurcated world of technology and
efficiency represented by the white peoples. The coming of the
railroad (a separating, fragmenting mechanism for the Indian,
the emblem of national unity for Sir John A. Macdonald) becomes
a potent symbol—in *The Scorched-Wood People* as well as here—
for the enormity of historical change and the enforced break-up of
a traditional way of life. Against this is set one of the last Indian
buffalo-runs. Big Bear's account of his vision of blood conveys an
extraordinary sense of "blood-intimacy" (D.H. Lawrence's term
alone comes close to capturing the effect here):

> A fountain of blood growing in the ground there like a
> prairie lily opening upwards and swelling higher as if it
> grew soft and thick, and higher so he put out his hand to stop
> that. For an instant the fountain died, sucked back to almost
> nothing as his fingers approached and then suddenly it burst
> up between them into his face and he had to fall back. The
> sky above him was flaming red, red slimed him completely,
> wherever he looked he saw all merging to red in the spray of
> the fountain. . . . The whole world had changed to blood.
> (130)

In this passage (which needs to be read in its entirety) Wiebe triumphantly succeeds in forcing his reader to respond as nineteenth-century Indian rather than as twentieth-century white man. He is able to present the scene wholly through Big Bear's consciousness, without any trace of our contemporary ecological concern. At moments like these we can understand what Maria Campbell, author of *Halfbreed,* meant when she claimed that the spirit of Big Bear took over from Wiebe and wrote the speeches for him (see *VL*, 151). His ability to control (indeed, to transform) our response, to prevent us however temporarily from recalling our habitual perspective, represents a masterly *tour de force.*

I need not, I think, reinforce my main point, since supporting examples abound in the rest of the novel. The vibrantly rhythmic prose that recreates the Indian Thirst Dance (III, iii) with its haunting reiterated phrase, "Big Bear was dancing" (163-4), contrasts dramatically—some might say, unfairly—with the statistical details, journalistic distortions, and prosaic vernacular of the white sections. This is doubtless part of what Wiebe means by acknowledging that "it's written in a very biased way," though his sympathetic presentation of such figures as Kitty McLean and James Simpson prevents this conscious bias from degenerating into an artistically damaging onesidedness. The contrast is particularly sharp, as might be expected, in the trial scene where Big Bear's imaginative eloquence sounds strange amid the legalistic rhetoric of magistrate and counsel. This dominant artistic strategy within the novel comes to a climax in Big Bear's final, confused, but movingly cogent vision of the developed prairie, all the more effective since the point is made credibly and appropriately through Big Bear's consciousness:

> He saw then that straight lines had squared up the land at right angles, broad lines of stark bleached bones had been spread straight, pressed and flattened into the earth for him to ride over, and sliced into hills as if that broad thong of bone could knuckle them down, those immoveable hills. As far as he could see, wherever he looked the world was slit open with unending lines, squares, rectangles of bone and

between the strange trees gleamed straight lines of, he
comprehended it suddenly, white buildings. Square inedible
mushrooms burst up under poplars overnight; but square.
He could not comprehend where he was. (409)

The land is "dead with no Thunderbird to revive it." The victory
of the white inhabitants in their white buildings is complete. *The
Temptations of Big Bear*, like *The Scorched-Wood People*, is an
elegy for a way of life.

Big Bear interests Wiebe for many reasons, but above all for
the religious attitude he represents. Because the whites do not
share his religious view of the earth but are concerned only with
its commercial and economic value, this is a quality that shows up
only fitfully, if at all, in the historical documents. Wiebe has
pointed out that, in the penitentiary records relating to Big Bear,
the Indian leader's religion is officially recorded as "None" (*VL*,
137). Wiebe insists, to the contrary, that Big Bear was a profoundly religious man, and that this went unrecognized not only
because it was out of line with the standard nineteenth-century
versions of Christian thought but also because it was *lived*. Big
Bear's religious principles manifested themselves continually in
the behaviour and attitudes of the whole man, instead of being
divided (like the land after the surveyors had completed their
work) into separate compartments. Hence the novel itself, though
less conspicuously religious than the earlier books, is no less so in
essence. As Wiebe remarked to Donald Cameron while *The
Temptations of Big Bear* was still being written, it "is totally non-
religious in a formal sense, and in another way it's fantastically
religious, because once you get to know what Indian people of
that time were like, they *were* and *are* more religious than you can
ever imagine a white man being."[9]

Big Bear's religion, however, is in no way transcendental;
though his god, "The First One" or "The Only One," is
mysterious and beyond, he is specifically the god of the Plains
Cree and the god of the land which they inhabit. Similarly Big
Bear himself, as chief, is inextricably associated with the land,

with sand and rock, and this association is not merely asserted as historical content but established metaphorically within the language of the novel. Throughout the book, the Indians and especially Big Bear are seen in terms of rock: "rock was the oldest, eternal grandfather of all things who stayed in his place and you could be certain of him. Whites were only certain in changing ..." (101). Later, Big Bear tells Kitty McLean the story of Bitter Spirit which Wiebe has recently described as "the myth told by almost every tribe in North America about their place."[10] Bitter Spirit asks of his divine host that he may live for ever and his request is, after a fashion, granted. In Big Bear's words: "He was transformed into rock. Rock gives us the pipe by which we pray to The First One, for rock is the grandfather of all, the first of all being as well as the last" (314-5).

These and other references unite in the last, magnificent paragraph in which Big Bear becomes in death the rocky land over which he has lived, hunted, and ruled:

> He felt the granular sand joined by snow running together, against and over him in delicate streams. It sifted over the crevices of his lips and eyes, between the folds of his face and hair and hands, legs; gradually rounded him over until there was a tiny mound on the sand hill almost imperceptible on the level horizon. Slowly, slowly, all changed continually into indistinguishable, as it seemed, and everlasting, unchanging, rock. (415)

All this may seem far removed from a Christian religious consciousness, but Wiebe's art depends, here as much as in his other novels, on the ever-present but not necessarily stated parallels with Biblical reference and structure. It is not illegitimate to recall here Psalm 18:2 ("The Lord is my rock, and my fortress, and my deliverer") or Christ's words to Peter in Matthew 16:18 ("upon this rock I will build my church"). Big Bear's "paganism," as we shall see, continually interconnects with Christian belief and symbolism.

Big Bear, then, is the dominating figure in the book; as John Moss has remarked, acutely, "whatever the perspective, Big Bear is always the central presence."[11] He is the key-figure for Wiebe's purpose because of all the Indians he was the one who best understood the situation of his race in the 1870s and 1880s and could most appropriately serve as spokesman for the Indian point of view. I have already quoted Wiebe's description of him as "an incredibly great man," but it is important to realize that he is in no way a hero in the conventional sense of the term. Wiebe told Ken Adachi that "the true hero is the man who affects us for eternity—not the conquering king but the suffering man."[12] Louis Riel was under discussion at the time, but the remark applies equally well to Big Bear. First of all, he is continually passive rather than active. He resists signing the treaty, he refuses to settle on a reservation, he has no wish to commit his followers to Riel and the Métis. Ironically (but aptly) his one action in the whole of the novel that could conceivably have some effect on events is his unsuccessful attempt to prevent the Frog Lake massacre. His tragedy (and he does, surely, rise to tragic heights in the course of the novel) lies in the fact that there is nothing he can do. Action, indeed, is one of the temptations alluded to in the title. Like all the Indians, he is caught between the temptation to submit to the hostile white methods and the temptation to rebellion and violence. As Frank Davey has written, "both these temptations offer nothing but ignoble sorts of deaths to the Cree culture."[13]

But the title, *The Temptations of Big Bear*, also inevitably suggests the temptations of Christ. Another irony seems present here, since Big Bear's attitude is unabashedly pagan, and he rejects the missionary activities of Catholic and Protestant alike (his acceptance of the Church at the close of the novel [409]—again an essentially passive acceptance—is a bitter token of his defeat). But the ultimate irony, for Wiebe, lies in the fact that Big Bear's "paganism," however distant from the forms and teachings of Christianity, is basically far closer to the message of Christ than the perfunctory pieties of the white characters in the novel. "Prayer and power" (195) are the two most important principles for Big Bear and the Indians. Big Bear is praying throughout the book, and just before his death reference is made to "the long prayer to The Only One that was his life" (414); power in this context is not the might-is-right ethic of the white man but inner strength, the quality Big Bear derives from The Only One through his power-bundle. Like Christ, Big Bear withstands his temptations, and he also resembles Christ in suffering for his people. "You will carry it all on your own back," James Simpson tells him after the killings at Frog Lake (267), and this proves as prophetic as Big Bear's own vision of hanged Cree warriors. He is not so much a hero, then, as a sacrificial victim.

Clearly, Wiebe is fascinated by Big Bear. His fellow-Albertan novelist, friend, and intellectual sparring partner, Robert Kroetsch, has spoken shrewdly of Wiebe's "uninventing himself back to Big Bear"[14] but a case could be made for an attempt at total sympathetic identification. When in New York Wiebe held Big Bear's power-bundle in his hands, and so came, by direct contact, as close as is now possible to the Indian chief, he offered up "a prayer to the Great Spirit who Big Bear, and I also, believe shaped the universe as He did for no other reason than that apparently He wanted to" (*VL*, 148). One senses here an aspiration towards complete rapport, and it is possible that some of Wiebe's own religious views have transferred themselves to Big Bear. Eli Mandel has remarked that in Big Bear's words he hears "not so much Indian speech, whatever that might be, but Biblical speech" (*VL*, 151-2), and one reviewer argued that "Big Bear's pacifism seems more native to Wiebe's Mennonite world than to Big Bear's Cree."[15]

These observations may or may not be valid. I mention them here because they give some substance to my belief that Wiebe more than most novelists—and, what may be closer to the point, even more than most *modern* novelists—seems to feel the need to identify himself closely with his principal characters. Thom Wiens and Joseph Dueck, and probably Hal Wiens in *Peace Shall Destroy Many,* contain certain aspects of their creator, and the same can be said for Abe Ross and Josh Bishop in *First and Vital*

Candle and John Reimer in *The Blue Mountains of China*. In the short stories, Bud and Andy, the Mennonite boys in "Scrapbook" and "Tudor King," are obviously drawn from memories of his own childhood, and the story-making narrators of "Bluecoats on the Sacred Hill of the Wild Peas" and "Where is the Voice Coming From?" are recognizable shadows of Rudy Wiebe himself. In a historical novel like *The Temptations of Big Bear*, the impulse towards imaginative identification is more difficult to attain or sustain, but I consider it an important part of the total effect, and shall be bringing forward evidence in my discussion of *The Scorched-Wood People* to suggest that Wiebe's relation with his leading character Riel and his ostensible mouthpiece Pierre Falcon is particularly complex. The point is of more than casual interest since it helps to explain the sense of almost uncanny immediacy that we feel in these books, as if author and character have entered into so intimate an imaginative partnership that each can inhabit the other's mind.

This kind of speculation carries us well beyond the normal boundaries of literary criticism. But even the brief raising of such speculation may be considered legitimate if it helps to explain some of the problems involved in responding adequately to the novel. There is no doubt, I think, that *The Temptations of Big Bear* raises considerable difficulties for the beginning reader; it is not easy to get to the point where the remarkable qualities of the novel can be appreciated. Many of these difficulties derive from the fact that little is generally known about Big Bear and his tribe, though the effect Wiebe requires in the novel depends upon the reader's full immersion into the life and experiences—and even, in Big Bear's case, the mind—of the Plains Cree. We must see, hear, feel, and even smell the members of Big Bear's tribe, and this entails our being exposed to a battery of unfamiliar names, strange words, and alien customs, and required to come to terms with them as best we may. The novelist cannot do the work for us. If we are ever to attain any deep understanding of the issues at stake, we must enter into the most intimate and complex details of a totally different way of life from our own. There are no half-measures. To adapt a phrase of Gabriel Dumont in *The Scorched-Wood People*, "to live here you have to think . . . Indian" (*SWP*, 213).

Wiebe seems to have been acutely conscious of this aesthetic difficulty while in the process of writing the book. In "On the Trail of Big Bear" he tells us that he originally wrote an introductory chapter containing "a sort of Henry Fielding narrator-type who hints at explanations in case his readers (whom I think he basically does not trust) don't catch on." It was to begin by reproducing the opening sentence of Hugh MacLennan's *The Watch That Ends the Night*: "There are some stories into which the reader should be led gently, and I think this may be one of them" (*VL*, 136). One can appreciate his difficulty, though so trickily sophisticated an effect as that is totally uncharacteristic of Wiebe, and we can readily concede that he was right to start again. There are some stories, indeed, in which the reader should *not* be led gently, and however we may grumble (as several of the initial reviewers did) about the difficulties we encounter in the book as it now stands, *The Temptations of Big Bear* is almost certainly one of them.

I once remarked to Wiebe that much of the reader's puzzlement came from his difficulty in distinguishing between the numerous Indians with their unfamiliar names. He retorted banteringly (doubtless with an eye on my surname) that they were much easier to distinguish than the white, usually Scots names, most of which began with "Mac."[16] There is, of course, much truth in this, but it sidesteps the basic problem. The average white reader, however willing, cannot but feel perplexed in this new environment, and the casual introduction of Big Bear's numerous wives and sons, not to mention the other chiefs and councillors, will only add to his confusion. The difficulty is a real one, but again it is intrinsic—essential—to the novel. A reader who has been bewildered by being plunged into a totally different society and way of life may be able, ultimately, to comprehend Big Bear's own confusion in an alien white world. As early as the second section he has expressed this sense of bewilderment: "Now I no longer understand and feel as once I understood when I did not see so many white men before me" (23). The phrase "I do not understand" is echoed again and again (see, for example, 30, 31, 32). Much of the pathos arising out of his trial derives from the old chief's lack of contact with all the procedures and assumptions of the white court. There we see Big Bear through Kitty McLean's eyes: "he couldn't possibly be so without comprehension of all things white" (387). Up to this point Kitty, of all the whites, has been closest to Big Bear, but ultimately even she comes to realize the gap between them—"understanding at last she could not understand him" (388).

Understanding, then, is at the root of the novel. Wiebe himself has succeeded in winning through to the state in which he can "think Indian," and as readers we must endeavour to do the same. In discussing *The Blue Mountains of China*, I tried to describe my response to a first reading of that novel: a sense of puzzlement, even confusion, but one that was accompanied with a recognition of enormous artistic power. Much the same can be said of *The Temptations of Big Bear*, though the difficulties are compounded by the fact that, for most of us, Indian life and behaviour is far more remote than the ways of the Mennonites. Moreover, it is impossible to forget completely that Wiebe is a white striving to reproduce the Indian viewpoint; there is a sense of *willed* sympathy here that, for this reader at least, prevents the total acceptance that can be given to *The Blue Mountains of China*. On the other hand, we cannot but admire the ambitious grasp of this novel. "Giant fiction" indeed, it is not afraid to make the utmost demands upon the reader's patience and engagement, even if it hardly presents the difficulties we encounter on first looking into, say, Faulkner's *The Sound and the Fury*. But with every rereading, if my experience is at all typical, *The Temptations of Big Bear* becomes clearer and more impressive. It is a book to be not so much read as lived with and grown into. Within the novel, Edgar Dewdney tells Sir John A. Macdonald that "old Big Bear has lived into his own understanding of that land" (115). Although it may be a slow and sometimes frustrating process, we must try to do the same for Wiebe's book. Above all, we should approach *The Temptations of Big Bear* with the same humility that, if we are sensible, we are accustomed to show in the presence of an acknowledged work of genius.

Although it magnificently creates its own world, *The Temptations of Big Bear* is an extension, intellectually and aesthetically rather than spatially or geographically, of his earlier work and not a departure from it. Frieda Friesen, too, lived into her own understanding of the land, and R.P. Bilan has recently demonstrated that "temptations" are also a recurring feature of *The Blue Mountains of China*.[17] Readers troubled by the strangeness of the Indian world here may draw reassurance from the continuities that are so important a feature of Wiebe's work. And, of course, the novel looks forward to *The Scorched-Wood People* in many important respects, not the least being the religious "vision" that provides a point of contact between Big Bear and Riel. But the most obvious point of resemblance is the identical chronological setting. In his next novel, Wiebe builds upon his first full-length experiment with historical fiction, and transcends the problem of "how you present facts"; indeed, he goes a long way towards attaining what he sees as the ideal for the historical novelist, the revelation that occurs when "a truly artistic intelligence subsumes all that fact for us and carries us with it beyond history."[18]

6 *The Scorched-Wood People*

After Big Bear, Riel. The development is logical enough; now
that we know, we recognize it as inevitable. Louis Riel has
haunted Rudy Wiebe's fiction from the beginning. He is mentioned in *Peace Shall Destroy Many* (see p. 26 above), in *First and
Vital Candle* Abe Ross visits his grave in Winnipeg (*FVC*, 45-6),
and although he never actually appears in *The Temptations of
Big Bear* he lurks intriguingly just off-stage. Another manifestation of the organic growth in Wiebe's writing may be found in the
larger pattern of progression from concern with his own Mennonite traditions to those of other minority groups dependent upon
the land: the Eskimos, the Indians, and now the Métis. None the
less, it would be a mistake to see *The Scorched-Wood People* as in
any facile sense a sequel to the previous novel. Wiebe recognizes
clearly the differences as well as the resemblances between the
situations of the Indians and the Métis. A remark that he made to
Donald Cameron in 1971, while *The Temptations of Big Bear* was
still being written, illustrates this distinction, and provides yet
another example of the constant development of his *oeuvre:* "I'm
working at [*The Temptations of Big Bear*] from the point of view
of what happened to the Indians at that time, which is really quite
different from what happened to the Métis, especially one like
Riel, who was educated as a white man and who never felt this
total kind of alienation, . . . of a totally foreign group moving in

and taking all his land away."[1] Wiebe has probably modified this view in the last few years—after all, a central theme of both books is expressed here by Riel himself as follows: "we must preserve for our children that liberty, that possession of soil, without which there is no happiness for anyone" (248). But whereas *The Temptations of Big Bear* presented an inevitable clash between the assumptions, attitudes, and methods of white and Indian, much of the tension in *The Scorched-Wood People* derives from conflicting impulses within Riel himself.

The historical Louis Riel offers himself as an ideal protagonist for Wiebe. His prairie birth and upbringing, his mixed (*métis*) blood linking him with both aboriginals and outsiders in his native place, his curious fusion of uncertain *naiveté* with vaunting ambition, his searing religious vision, the violent passion lurking just beneath the surface of his consciousness: all these qualities, explored separately by Wiebe elsewhere, here combine in a single, inevitably "epic" figure. Moreover, history provided Wiebe not only with this unique and complex character but with abundant archival records and conflicting interpretations to stimulate his artistic impulse. For good or ill, Riel haunts the Canadian consciousness, provoking reactions ranging from embittered rejection to uncritical hero-worship. Whether hailed as religious and political leader or condemned as fanatic and madman, he remains a fascinating enigma whose personality and behaviour can be explored in depth but never ultimately fathomed.

Wiebe takes pains to present him sympathetically but not uncritically. Part of the attraction of this fictional but meticulously researched portrait is that he proves as elusive in fiction as in life. No one can read the book without receiving an unforgettable impression of the mystery that was Louis Riel, but although he dominates the novel he is not, in the strictest sense, its centre. While he appears on one level as a heroic individual, on another he is the epic representative of his race, the *bois-brûlés* or "scorched-wood people." This is the story, primarily, of the rise and fall of a nation. And in artistic terms the challenge and fascination of the book stem not so much from the presentation of the leading character (since Wiebe's Riel is ultimately no more and no less inscrutable than the Riel of history) as from the manifold problems of historical fiction, the uneasy relations between epic and novel, the analogues with Biblical structure, the fluctuating position of the narrator (where the voice comes from). For this reason (and also because, with a book of these proportions, one must necessarily be selective) I shall be concentrating here less on the perplexing and entrancing figure of Riel himself than on the literary problems associated with Wiebe's depiction of him.

Like its predecessor, this novel is a "big" book—what Wiebe called "giant fiction"—not only in terms of numbers of pages but in its scope, its implications, and the multiplicity of its themes. Wiebe's problem was to find a form that could adequately contain all that he wanted to present, and this is reflected in the difficulty he seems to have experienced in finding a suitable title. We know that he once thought of calling it *Riel and Gabriel,* and in some prepublication material the novel was announced as *Northwest to Batoche.* The final choice, *The Scorched-Wood People,* was probably the best (*Riel and Gabriel* implies a character-balance that is not attempted in the novel, and *Northwest to Batoche,* though dramatic, suggests Hollywood rather than seriousness), but its emphasis on the Métis rather than on their leader could encourage the reader to expect a simpler structure than the book offers. Even more than *The Temptations of Big Bear, The Scorched-Wood People* can be fruitfully considered not only as historical fiction but as epic and as tragedy. The three can often conflict but are not in themselves mutually exclusive. The result, in Wiebe's now experienced hands, is a narrative with a remarkably complex structure.

The Scorched-Wood People is as meticulously researched as *The Temptations of Big Bear,* and there is a comparable if less conspicuous emphasis on documents and historical exactitude. But the informative element is less pressing here. As we have seen, Wiebe was stimulated to write about Big Bear not only because of his fascination with the Indian chief but also because Big Bear's story was "almost totally unknown" (*VL*, 154). By contrast, however, all literate Canadians know something about Riel, his presidency of the provisional government after the seizure of Fort Garry in 1869, the controversial shooting of Thomas Scott, his flight on the arrival of Wolseley's military force from Ontario, his return to what is now Saskatchewan in 1884, the defeat at Batoche in the following year, his trial and execution. We do not read *The Scorched-Wood People* for information but for elucidation and understanding. What Wiebe has to combat here is not ignorance but prejudice.

As I noted in the previous chapter, up to the time of publishing *The Temptations of Big Bear*, Wiebe had accepted the common assumption that history is "written impartially" (*VL*, 152).[2] However, as soon as he began to conduct research into the events culminating in the Riel rebellions, he must have developed considerable doubts on the matter. The impartiality of the historian, he came to realize, is a pious hope rather than an achieved fact. Hartwell Bowsfield's gathering of literature on the subject in the "Issues in Canadian History" series is aptly if ponderously entitled *Louis Riel. Rebel of the Western Frontier or Victim of Politics and Prejudice?* (1969). Not long after the publication of *The Scorched-Wood People*, Wiebe himself wrote an article for the *Toronto Globe and Mail* under the heading, "In the west, Sir John A. is a bastard and Riel a saint. Ever ask why?" Both titles make the same point: the story of Riel changes drastically with the presuppositions that are brought to bear upon it.

Moreover, differences of interpretation are not necessarily explained by the quality and training of the historian. A convenient illustration (one that Wiebe may well have encountered while preparing to write *The Scorched-Wood People*) is to be found in no less prestigious a place than Donald Creighton's *John A. Macdonald: The Old Chieftain* (winner of the Governor-General's award for non-fiction in 1955). On p. 67, in the section dealing with Riel's provisional government at Red River, we are told that "the military expedition, with its complement of British regulars and with Colonel Garnet Wolseley as its commander, was about to leave for Red River, and a political settlement of the north-west had finally been achieved in the Manitoba Bill." We hear nothing more about this until p. 73 when we come upon the following: " . . . in the west the territorial expansion of the new Dominion was about to be triumphantly completed. The Red River military expedition had reached its objective without incident, and had confirmed British-Canadian occupation of the north-west." Wolseley's orders, the collapse of the provisional government and the circumstances surrounding it, Riel's enforced flight to the United States, all these are glossed over, despite the fact that the authority, aims, and actions of Wolseley's expedition are essential factors if we are to come to terms with Macdonald's political morality and strategy at this period. Creighton's method may just qualify as objective (he certainly writes from a distanced perspective, and nothing he states is actually false), but it can hardly be called impartial. And this kind of distortion is not, of course, a prerogative of anti-Riel historians. In Peter Charlebois's sympathetically partisan *Life of Louis Riel* (1975), the manipulations of rhetoric include even such crude effects as referring to Riel's "supporters" but to Schultz's "gang."[3] Once again, historical impartiality is flouted.

The most detailed and least biased account of Riel's life and activities is George F.G. Stanley's *Louis Riel* (1963), praised by Wiebe in 1974 as "the only good biography written to date."[4] But, admirable as it is, this is a book for the specialist historian, and may well prove too intricate and academic for the general reader. Wiebe, though appreciative of thorough scholarship, is himself concerned to bring Riel's story to life, to interpret its significance for as wide a reading public as possible, and the book that has clearly had the greatest influence on his own work is Joseph Kinsey Howard's *Strange Empire: A Narrative of the Northwest* (1952). Howard was an American, resident in Montana, whose early experience straddled the American-Canadian border not unlike Wallace Stegner's. A posthumous publication, *Strange*

Empire was seen through the press by Bernard de Voto, who praises Howard in the introduction because "he is not a sympathetic white man depicting the Métis and the Cree: he has become a Métis or a Cree,"[5] an observation recalling Maria Campbell on Wiebe and Big Bear. More important, however, is the fact that this is a popular history, learned and knowledgeable to be sure, but told with emphasis on the dramatic aspects of the narrative, and concentrating on the broad sweep of events rather than on the minutiae of academic detail. Above all, in "becoming a Métis," Howard views the material with the kind of impassioned bias that we saw Wiebe assign to the approach of the artist rather than that of the historian; the book had already, indeed, been a significant influence on Don Gutteridge's *Riel: A Poem for Voices*, first published in 1968. Wiebe's own presentation of the material also resembles Howard's, but his fictional approach allows him a greater imaginative licence.

Because the broad outlines of Riel's story are far more familiar than those of Big Bear, then, Wiebe does not feel so closely bound in this novel to what Georg Lukács, the historian of the historical novel, calls "the cult of facts."[6] He has learned that "unless they are very carefully handled, facts are invariably the tyrants of story" (*VL*, 132-3). History is now "adapted" with more confidence, consciously shaped to point up the pattern behind events. The whole problem is transcended to some extent by the choice of narrator, the Métis poet Pierre Falcon who obviously introduces "bias" into the telling, but I shall consider the artistic implications of this device at a later stage in my discussion. Here it is important to face up to the matter of historical accuracy and to consider Wiebe's practice in relation to the recognized and accepted rules that govern historical fiction.

In what way does Wiebe depart from historical accuracy? Most obviously, in a telescoping of incident that results in a heightening of dramatic tension. This is particularly evident in the opening chapter, where events that took place at Fort Garry between early December 1869 and mid-February 1870—the proclamation of the provisional government, the raising of the flag, the escape of the Canadian prisoners, the deaths of Sutherland and Parisien—are contracted into a single day. As a result, Riel is often styled "President" on occasions (and even in adapted documents) before he actually held that office. Moreover, Thomas Scott is made directly responsible for Parisien's death in a manner not fully confirmed by the historical evidence. Wiebe also takes liberties with the historical record in his presentation of Gabriel Dumont. As George Woodcock pointed out in a rather unsympathetic review, Dumont was not "present at the Red River throughout the period of Riel's ascendancy" and did not in fact witness the repulsing of McDougall and the execution of Thomas Scott.[7]

Historians will be troubled (and, from their own stance, properly so) by these divergencies from the surviving evidence, but it cannot be emphasized too strongly that Wiebe is writing historical fiction and must be judged by the appropriate criteria. Since serious historical fiction does not yet form a prominent part of Canadian literature, its conventions are not as well known as they might be, and I must therefore set Wiebe's practice within the context of the earlier development of his chosen genre. Georg Lukács' *The Historical Novel* (1937; trans. 1962) remains the most detailed and comprehensive work on this subject, and repays study despite the self-imposed Marxist blinkers through which he persists in viewing his material. The essential characteristics he requires of the genre may be summarized as follows: correlation between "the individuality of characters" and "the historical peculiarity of the age"; portrayal of "the totality of national life in its complex interaction between 'above' and 'below' "; "bringing the past to life as the prehistory of the present"; and, above all, the subordination of "individual facts" in the interests of "a deeper fidelity to the spirit of the whole."[8] The function of the historical novelist, then, is to catch the essence of a historical event, which is generally a crucial turning-point in the fortunes of the nation or nations involved. Lukács argues that, paradoxical as it may at first seem, an excess of historical authenticity and an over-reliance on carefully researched detail is likely to defeat the purpose of historical fiction since it will emphasize rather than minimize the distinction between historical subject-matter and contemporary situation and so fail to establish the all-important human rapport between historical characters and modern readers. "The 'cult of facts'," Lukács insists, "is a miserable surrogate for this intimacy with the people's historical life."[9]

Few, I suppose, are likely to object to the concentration and telescoping of events, since little or no distortion is involved in speeding up the more leisurely pace of history. The account of the death of Parisien is a more serious divergence, in time, in detail, and in ascribing the full blame to Thomas Scott, but the Canadian party was none the less collectively responsible, and Scott's character is ultimately little affected by Wiebe's exaggeration of his contemptible behaviour. The presentation of Gabriel Dumont is more controversial. Given George Woodcock's admiration for Dumont, and his detailed knowledge of his biography as evidenced by *Gabriel Dumont: The Métis Chief and His Lost World* (1975), it is not perhaps surprising that he should emphasize Wiebe's departure from historical accuracy in this instance. None the less, I am surprised to find him not only judging *The Scorched-Wood People* almost exclusively in terms of its factual reliability, but apparently unable to comprehend the reasons for Wiebe's "distortions." "For some reason which is not evident," he writes, "Wiebe has Dumont continually present during the months of provisional government at Fort Garry."[10] I would have thought, on the contrary, that the reason was obvious enough. Wiebe sees the whole action in terms of the conflicting claims of organized violence and religious vision. Dumont was, after all, the main strategist of Métis resistance, and his deference to Riel's idealistic faith at Batoche if not at Red River is historically documented, most eloquently, indeed, by Woodcock himself. Wiebe sees the need to point up the contrast between the two leaders, partly to offset the danger of sentimentalizing the situation by offering a simplified White violence/Métis visionary dichotomy, partly to create in Riel and Dumont comprehensive emblems of the Métis dilemma. (Woodcock himself describes Riel as "the prophet" and Dumont as "the man of action."[11]) Personally, I find Wiebe's Dumont more complex and much more sympathetic than the "crude and violent" figure discovered and rejected by Woodcock.[12] His fluctuation between revengeful bitterness and a tough materialism on the one hand and (under the influence of Riel) a willed patience and sudden religious awareness on the other seems to me both moving and deeply human, and, however untypical it may or may not be of the historical Dumont, by no means unrepresentative of many of his Métis followers.[13]

Wiebe conforms, I think, to all Lukács' *major* requirements for "classic" historical fiction. Certainly, his characters come across as fully believable yet they are decidedly Métis figures of the nineteenth century rather than modern men and women in fancy dress. Equally certainly, we experience (as we did in *The Temptations of Big Bear*) a sharp sense of "the totality of national life" since Wiebe ranges at will between Sir John A. Macdonald and Sir George-Etienne Cartier, Riel and Dumont, Bishop Taché and Father Ritchot, Scott and Schultz, Patrice Tourond and Napoléon Nault, etc. etc. Again, the continuity of past and present, the sense that we inherit, albeit indirectly, the consequences of the events about which Wiebe writes, is always apparent. These nineteenth-century scenes are continually exploding into the painfully contemporary: the future of Quebec ("vive le North-West libre" [31]), the pipeline debate ("Until then Ottawa apparently did not know that there were people in the North-West who must be talked with before they are disposed of" [59]). Such echoes reach a culmination in the sardonic epilogue where Dumont encounters Lief Crozier, late of the Mounted Police, while performing in Buffalo Bill's Wild West Show in New York. Dumont reports Riel as saying, "a hundred years is just a spoke in the wheel of eternity" (351), and comments: "A hundred years, and whites still won't know what to do with him" (351). The appearance of the novel almost exactly a century after the events it describes drives home the point. In Wiebe there is no artificial gap between past and present.

There are, however, various places where Wiebe's practice

conflicts with Lukács' norms. (This is hardly surprising since Lukács is basing his generalizations on what has been achieved, and realizes that new situations will give birth to new artistic possibilities.) Perhaps the most interesting of these is Lukács' insistence that, in the classic historical novel, authentic leaders (whom he calls, rather chillingly, "world-historical individuals") should never occupy a central position but should appear only as minor characters. Lukács considers this a feature of the novel as distinct from either epic or tragic drama. Although these last may focus upon the inner conflicts of major figures (Achilles, Aeneas, Coriolanus, Henry IV), fiction by its very nature emphasizes the social, communal nature of historical forces. The novel, he claims, sees the historical leader (Scott's Bonnie Prince Charlie and Rob Roy, Tolstoy's Napoleon—and Kutuzov) as culminations of vast historical trends, not individuals who impose their own visions upon their followers. Lukács has dialectical objections to the cult of personality, and rejects literary instances as the false fruits of Romantic reaction.

At the same time, however, Lukács grants that "the all-national character of the principal themes of epic, the relation between individual and nation in the age of heroes require that the most important figure should occupy the central position, while in the historical novel he is necessarily only a minor character."[14] This is interesting because there are many features of Wiebe's later fiction that belong to epic more than to the conventional novel. Lukács writes, for instance, of Scott's "selection of those periods and those strata of society which embody the old epic self-activity of man, the old epic directness of social life, its public spontaneity."[15] It is not difficult for readers of *The Temptations of Big Bear* and *The Scorched-Wood People* to see Wiebe's books as illustrating Lukács' point even more clearly than *Waverley* or *Old Mortality*.

Indeed, when we come to articulate the difference between reading Wiebe and reading other modern novelists, we may well isolate a sense of epic expansiveness, the presentation of a more primitive world of action and individual achievement in which heroic behaviour is still possible and even customary. Moreover, the historic confrontations in Wiebe's later work invariably take the form of conflicts between the values of epic and those of modern *Realpolitik*. Sweetgrass's signing of the treaty at the opening of *The Temptations of Big Bear* symbolizes the acceptance, by all but the epically conceived Big Bear, that the world of heroic action is doomed. And in *The Scorched-Wood People* Riel proves to be helpless in a modern political situation in which oral governmental promises can be revoked if it proves inexpedient to honour them, and apparently eternal systems can be expunged by the measurements of a theodolite or the driving home of a last spike. This last example is particularly crucial: "the railroad," Falcon is made to observe, "had forever destroyed any space west" (191). Both novels contain moving scenes in which the coming of the railroad is presented as symbolic of a catastrophic change in local habits, fortunes, and attitudes. Wiebe makes the relevant point even more succinctly in a satirical outburst in his essay "On the Trail of Big Bear": "oh, the heroism of that 19th century computer Van Horne as sung by that 20th century computer Pierre Berton Incorporated!" (*VL*, 134). In *The Temptations of Big Bear* and *The Scorched-Wood People* he presents the other, more genuine form of heroism that was being displaced.

The Scorched-Wood People is epic in other ways too. As I have already noted, it differs from most novels in presenting, literally, the story of the rise and fall of a nation. The phrase "New Nation," conspicuously capitalized, rings poignantly throughout the book (see 25, 60, 185, 219, 310, 313, 344, 348). And the nation dies with its hero. Its epitaph is spoken by the spirit of Pierre Falcon immediately following the scene of Riel's execution:

That is all the story I can tell you. Our New Nation blossomed and faded for a few short months in Manitoba in 1869-70, it blazed up in 1885 and in less than two months died on the Saskatchewan. Our prairie vision was too strong, too destructive of all that was; it had to be borne away by the violent. (348)

There is, in fact, a characteristically epic effect (one thinks of Greek Homer lamenting the fall of Troy, or the *Beowulf*-poet singing the praises of the Geat hero in Old English) in the presentation of Canadians as the enemy in this most ambitious and expansive of Canadian fictions. Sir John A. Macdonald is the nation-builder; but the epic hero is Riel, "the man who had to hang."

Pierre Falcon, Métis song-maker, is an appropriate narrator for *The Scorched-Wood People*, even if the historical composer of scurrilous songs ("my silly, ironic, ribald songs," he calls them [322]) must be elevated by Wiebe into an epic poet. Certainly his presence as venerated bard at the Red River celebrations in the first chapter conjures up an authentic heroic atmosphere. And although his commentary ranges from heroic (and novelistic) narrative, through elegiac lament, to a somewhat problematic historical analysis, the authentic epic voice is always latent, to be invoked whenever needed. A particularly memorable instance occurs at the opening of the fatal last day of the battle at Batoche:

> Between the first and second line of rifle pits were killed Michel Trottier, André Batoche, Calixte Tourond and his brother Elzéar, two Sioux warriors, all by bayonet; José Vandal who had both arms broken first and then was finished off by bayonet; Donald Ross and Isidore Boyer, both over seventy-five and killed by bayonet; John Swan, and also Démase Carrière, shooting until his rifle was empty and then clubbing the red soldiers bellowing over him as his leg was shattered by a ball....(304)

Even readers unfamiliar with the conventions of traditional epic will recognize that a peculiarly primitive effect is being achieved here, and Wiebe has acknowledged in the course of at least one public reading (Calgary, February 1978) that this is his equivalent of the customary epic list. His remark proves, if proof were needed, that the epic quality in the book is a result of the novelist's deliberate art.

There is, however, a third traditional element that combines with those of epic and historical novel as a slighter but none the less palpable ingredient in *The Scorched-Wood People*: that of dramatic tragedy. Not that there is any question of a strictly formal resemblance; rather, the very nature of the story invites us to think of it in dramatic terms. John Coulter's example in dramatizing Riel's trial was available to Wiebe at the time he wrote (he mentions both *Riel* and *The Trial of Louis Riel* with respect as early as 1971[16]), though Wiebe's greater imaginative power causes his own Riel to seem more essentially dramatic a character than Coulter's. Many of the scenes (the Red River celebration, the public clash with the delegates at the Court House, Riel's overhearing the conversation between Wolseley and John Kerr, the trial itself—this last foreshortened, I presume, because of the lengthy trial-scene at the end of *The Temptations of Big Bear*) have theatrical or cinematographic qualities that blend readily enough with the epic tone. Wiebe's interesting and consistent stylization of Michel Dumas into the traditional role of tragic messenger (see 66, 114, 222, 282) is another device that has its origins in drama.[17]

Equally dramatic, but less compatible with epic treatment, is an emphasis on the doomed hero that is not only personal but psychological. The scenes in exile, especially those at the time of his mental breakdown, examine Riel's inner conflicts, comparing and contrasting these with his active struggles and defeats. In providing extracts from Riel's diary jottings and reconstructing his inmost thoughts, Wiebe offers the intimate revelation of his hero's mind in a way that recalls traditional soliloquy. Again, his sister Sara's summing-up of Riel's situation, "You are suffering enough, as if all the sins of our people, forgive me, you carry them like a scapegoat" (127), has overtones that associate it with dramatic ritual. Her words are truer than she knows; the pattern of Riel's life suggests a mysterious association between his own fortunes and those of his race, though by a tragic irony Riel's death coincides with that of his nation instead of being a surrogate for it. His people survive individually but not collectively; their corporate identity is inextricably bound up with his existence as their leader and spokesman. In this way his story naturally and inevitably attracts the communal emotion at the core of tragedy.

But Sara's allusion to the scapegoat, with its reference back to Leviticus 16:20-21, alerts us to yet another traditional strand within Wiebe's novel: the continual analogies that are offered between the account of Riel and the Métis on the one hand and the story, structure, and imagery of the Bible on the other. These range from broad thematic patterning (Riel's flight to and return from the United States suggesting the paradigm of Exodus) through the associations of individual scenes (Riel, like his prototype David, dancing before the Lord [163]) and the conscious links made within the story (Riel's identification of the Indians with the lost tribes of Israel [159]) to specific Biblical quotation (especially Riel's own quoting from the Psalms [160-1, 187, etc.]).

This is, of course, one of Wiebe's favourite narrative techniques, and it can be documented from all his novels. But the effect is magnified here because the associations are recognized (and, often, deliberately engineered) by the leading protagonist. Riel continually sees the events of his life in scriptural terms, and Wiebe, by emphasizing this, not only sets the history of the scorched-wood people *sub specie aeternitatis* but establishes hints of a divine plan reflected both in Riel's attempted creation of a Métis state and in the novelist's relation to his created artistic world. A subtle connection is thus set up between author and hero—one to which Wiebe drew attention when he remarked to George Melnyk, "What made me dare [tackle Riel] is that Riel was soaked in theology, as I am."[18] This is an important effect within the total experience of the novel and one to which I shall return. First, however, it is necessary to ask the question: how does Wiebe combine these historic, epic, dramatic, and scriptural strands into a unified work of art?

As I have already hinted, his chief means of reconciling the diverse elements out of which the book is formed involved the creation of the separate and quasi-historical narrator, Pierre Falcon, though this decision raised some problems while solving others. I write "quasi-historical" because, as most reviewers noted (though with drastically different reactions), Falcon's narrative is made to extend beyond the date of his own death, which occurred in 1876. Wiebe makes no secret of this—Falcon discusses his own funeral at one point (284)—but there can be no question, I think, that readers (including sympathetic and careful readers) can find the effect distracting while they are in the process of coming to terms with its challenge. For George Woodcock, "the idea of his continuing as a spectral narrator strains one's credence to the wrenching point."[19] In my view, this is by no means an unreasonable response to a first reading; the more familiar one becomes with the novel, however, the more one realizes the advantages of the device. Falcon's narration is, I am convinced, the crucial aesthetic issue in the novel, and it therefore demands to be discussed at some length.

The Scorched-Wood People is the first of Wiebe's full-length works to employ a single narrator, and the most obvious reason for his using the method here is that his interest in Riel's story demands a Métis'-eye-view. His detailed research into the literary treatment of Riel over the past century would undoubtedly have impressed upon him the importance of personal viewpoint in assessing Riel's actions and motives. Independent witness to the range of response has recently been offered by Dick Harrison. Riel, he reports, "became a villain of a particularly deep dye because his was a resistance which threatened the basic vision of order."[20] One only has to compare this with Falcon's summing-up already quoted—"Our prairie vision was too strong, too destructive of all that was; it had to be borne away by the violent" (348)—to understand how totally opposed verdicts can arise from identical premises. Harrison shows how, from J.E. Collins's irresponsible pot-boiler romances, *The Story of Louis Riel* (1885) and *Annette the Métis Spy* (1886), to as comparatively recent a book as Edward McCourt's *Flaming Hour* (1947) where Riel is described physically in terms that conjure up a picture of Adolf Hitler, Riel remained a villain in the West for generations.[21] For Wiebe (who has himself described Collins's work as catering to "eastern prejudice and ignorance"[22]) it was clearly time to right the balance.

The advantages of a Métis narrator now become obvious. But why Falcon, given the fact that he died nine years before the culmination of Riel's story? Primarily, of course, because he is the one well-known Métis poet, and Wiebe realized that the visionary aspect of the story required poetic presentation. Falcon, after all, had been present at the Seven Oaks massacre in 1816, and his song of victory, most accessible to English-speaking readers in James Reaney's version "Le Tombeau de Pierre Falcon," is a celebration of the birth of "Our Nation." Technically, it was possible for the lifespan of one man to extend from 1816 to 1885 and thus to see the first and the last of the Métis as a potential political and social unit; in Wiebe's novel Old Ouellette appears as a historical figure who achieved this sad distinction: "I've lived long enough . . . longer than our nation" (305). To have Falcon recount the story as if from a Métis heaven, looking down at the whole pattern of the action from the perspective of a Homeric god, not only reproduces a situation consonant with epic form but allows him to function as a representation of the spirit of all the Métis. Moreover, the disembodied stance is related to Wiebe's alteration and adaptation of historical detail. The interpretation Falcon offers, though in no serious way a distortion, is less a meticulous account of what happened than a comprehensive presentation of what the Métis see as having happened. Through the mouth of Falcon the poet we watch history in the process of turning, as it always does, into myth.

But we can go further. Within the novel, Pierre Falcon is invaluable as a mediator between facts and people. Possessing the vision of a poet, he is capable of understanding Riel better than his fellow-Métis; he can both articulate and explain the peculiar quality of Riel that his followers sensed but could never fathom.

Riel's respect for "Grandfather" Falcon (36) in the opening chapter includes a realization that Falcon as poet is a necessary spokesman. "Grandfather, how long must one live before he can speak for the dead?" he asks, and years afterward Dumont will overhear his paraphrasing Psalm 137: "of us who were carried away captive is required a song" (187). Falcon, in turn, offers the product of his art to his Métis companions as "a song we might sing, to help you remember" (38). Later in his narrative, when Riel is in enforced exile, Falcon will intervene to exclaim: "Remember us, Louis, remember your Métis people. For we will never forget you" (167). Remembrance is mutual, and we should not forget at this point that Riel is himself a poet; his sister Sara calls him "our singer-king" (129) when she inscribes "Louis David Riel" in her prayer-book, recalling David not merely as king but as poet of Israel. That Riel's own poems were themselves feeble is not at issue; Falcon knows that Riel's poetic vision had to be embodied in action, and he quotes Riel's aphorism, "True prophets are known by what they do" (250).

Falcon also serves, I think, as a consciously-created mediator between Riel and Wiebe himself. As a spokesman for the Métis, Falcon can be acknowledged as closer to his subject than Wiebe (or his readers) can ever be, a condition that makes for intimacy and authority; at the same time, he is himself distanced from Wiebe (and his readers), a condition that allows for, though does not of course guarantee, authorial objectivity. He is not the conspicuous narrator of most first-person fiction; he is at best a spectator, never (unless we count his composition and recital of "The Sad Ballad of King Muck-Dougall"[23]) a participant. Wiebe clearly hopes to enjoy the benefits of the multiple viewpoint he had used in *The Temptations of Big Bear* (Macdonald's discussion with Cartier, for example, performs a similar function to the letter from Dewdney to Macdonald in the earlier novel), but he also wants the immediacy and credibility that only an individual—and, more specifically, a Métis—witness could provide. Strictly speaking, I suppose, the two viewpoints are mutually exclusive; Wiebe can achieve the combination only by assigning

Falcon a privileged perspective in an omniscient Métis heaven.

Because Falcon is a fluctuating and (by the customary expectations of realism) inconsistent narrator, the reader may well encounter some initial difficulty in adjusting to what is in fact a new fictional convention. True, the epigraph to the novel begins with the lines,

> *And who has made this song?*
> *Who else but good Pierre Falcon,*

but the literal application of this to the narrative mode of the novel is unlikely to register at so early a stage. In the opening few pages the speaker seems to be a casual Métis observer at the proclamation at Red River in 1869. Only later is he unequivocally identified as Falcon, and even then the reader accustomed to Wiebe's shifts of narrator in *The Blue Mountains of China* and *The Temptations of Big Bear* may well assume that he is only a temporary spokesman. Later he is found to draw upon information and attitudes that he could not have possessed (Macdonald and Cartier discussing the situation in Ottawa, Schultz agitating in Toronto), and he generalizes upon events as if from a detached position in historical time. It is difficult at first to accept a convention whereby Falcon can speak as an eye-witness (like Old Ouellette who fought at Frog Plain and dies at Batoche) but also with the historical knowledge and twentieth-century experience of a Rudy Wiebe.

The desirability of combining both perspectives is evident. Wiebe needs the sense of personal immediacy (this is a story of "our people"), but he also needs the distanced overview that sees the Riel "rebellions" as doomed by larger historical forces that can be understood though not condoned—the viewpoint, in Stegner's words already quoted, of one "who can see the last years of the Plains frontier with the distance of history and with the passion of personal loss and defeat."[24] Yet Falcon's individual presence fades for pages at a time, and the intervening voice sounds more like that of a modern "objective" historian. Wiebe takes a considerable risk here; he asks his reader to accept a decidedly unusual authorial convention that demands an effort of both imagination and understanding. But if the reader is prepared to make this effort, the rewards are considerable.

For one thing, much of the effectiveness of the novel derives from a viewpoint that is relentlessly *sub specie aeternitatis*. "God's time is not ours," says the condemned Riel to Father Fourmond (326), and Falcon's narrative clearly aspires to God's time. The future is continually casting its shadow upon the past, as the opening sentence of the whole book testifies: "Sixteen years later Louis Riel would be dressing himself again, just as carefully" (10). The moment is recalled at the close (344) and functions as one of many similar structural frames. Most conspicuous of these, perhaps, is the continual anticipation of execution, especially the burning of the effigy in Wolseley's camp (120) and the joint revelation of Riel and Dumont on emerging from the church at Fort Benton: "a gallows there and a man swinging from that gallows" (188). Even Scott's execution is deliberately connected with Riel's in the echo, obvious enough but none the less effective, of the Lord's Prayer (87, 346). Telling the story through the omniscient spirit of Pierre Falcon, though awkward in other ways, makes these effects possible.

I have already noted that Riel and Wiebe and, to a lesser extent, Falcon, are linked by a preoccupation with the visionary. "Vision," indeed, is a major element not only in the subject-matter and vocabulary but even in the structure of the book. The word itself reverberates in expanding meanings through the novel: "the agony of the humiliation exploding into vision at the altar" (49); "belief in vision for which the mud on their feet gives them no evidence" (140); "for that vision I am chained here" (160); "in the Church I have seen visions of God sweeter than the flesh of Jesus on my tongue after confession" (202); "the light of his vision shone like a single fire blazing in a night storm" (273); "Vision God gave, and sometimes miracle" (301); etc., etc. The whole novel is summed up, indeed, in Falcon's phrase, "Riel's great vision" (245). Moreover, throughout the book characters are continually experiencing visionary glimpses of the future. In addition to the anticipation of Riel's execution, these include Father Ritchot at the Fort Garry celebrations, "his face gradually pulled together in agony as if he already saw ahead through four Indian fours of years to this very December day in St. Boniface Cathedral when he would be praying again surrounded by several thousand kneeling inside and out among the snowy stones of the cemetery; a coffin nailed shut within a ring of these very men" (24). Falcon himself later in the day sees "Canadians celebrating," the "arch of white Confederation ... already complete, ... the North-West tight against Ontario and Quebec, forever" (44); Riel, as Elzéar Goulet brings in Thomas Scott, is presented as seeing "Scott's body dangling, stretched tiptoe for the ground as that huge arm lifted" (74); Dumont, as the Métis force their horses across the newly-laid railroad tracks, physically shudders with a vague sense of "that moment as premonition" (194). Vision, we might say, has become structure. Falcon's "making" of his song of Riel depends upon his apprehending the whole of it from a position outside clock-time, like Wiebe himself.[25]

There is a sense, indeed, in which Falcon and Wiebe can be seen to have virtually coalesced by the end of the novel. In the opening section, Falcon insists:

> Let me tell you immediately, Louis Riel was a giant. If God had willed it, he could have ruled the world.
>   No, no, hear me out, and you will believe it too. (36)

By the end of the novel, I suggest, Falcon has persuaded (or come close to persuading) the reader and, one is tempted to add, the author. At first, we are conscious of Falcon's partiality as one narrating from within the events portrayed—immediately after the passage just quoted, Riel addresses Falcon and the Muck-Dougall ballad is introduced. But when Falcon speaks "from beyond the grave" (284) as an authoritative, omniscient narrator, he has taken over the function of the novelist; author and narrator can no longer be easily separated. When, for example, the narrator observes of a detail concerning Riel's trial, "I know of no historian who has commented on this . . . " (316), or interrupts his account of Riel arguing with his lawyers just before the trial to say, "It has always seemed to me that Riel made a mistake here" (321), there is no need to try to persuade ourselves that the speaker is Falcon rather than Wiebe. The distinction between them, that was once necessary for Wiebe's effect, is now transcended in the need for a unified response. This technique is daring, and perhaps not fully achieved, but the slight blurring of narrative clarity that it entails is surely a small price to pay for the expansion of imaginative vision that it makes possible.

The resultant coalescing of the viewpoints of author, narrator, and protagonist is hinted at in an important passage just before Batoche. Falcon asserts: "I could never make songs about an idea: a happening or a person was all I was ever given to sing in the long years of my life . . . and you had to think like Riel and see the exact problem standing where you could reach out your hand and touch it as Gabriel must in order to understand Duck Lake and Fish Creek and Batoche" (276). Falcon, Wiebe, Riel, and even Dumont all interconnect here, as they do implicitly throughout the book. Wiebe comes so close to imaginatively identifying himself with Riel that at one point he offers as a boyhood memory of Riel an incident that he elsewhere recounts as an auto-biographical experience of his own.[26] And part of the painful urgency behind the last half of the novel stems, I suggest, from the fact that Wiebe wants to believe in Riel's impossible "great vision" rather than Dumont's practical guerrilla-tactics, yet knows at the same time that, pragmatically, the latter were necessary for success. Once again peace and violence, Riel's cross and Dumont's rifle, coexist at the heart of the novel, and Wiebe, partly because he understands the attraction of both, exploits the creative possibilities of this paradox to their fullest extent.

I have tried in this discussion of *The Scorched-Wood People* to indicate something of the impressive richness to be found in the book. However, it is a richness seldom accompanied by formal elegance; there is a roughness and jaggedness about this novel (as, for that matter, about all Wiebe's work) that can offend devotees of artistic decorum. The qualities prominent in Wiebe's fiction—amplitude, sudden insight, exuberant creativity, emotional power—are all too likely to burst any mould that attempts to contain them. There is so much in *The Scorched-Wood People*, so many effects demanding attention, so many themes jostling for expression, that the reader may well find himself bewildered, overwhelmed by an embarrassment of riches. Historical novel, epic narrative, dramatic tragedy, Métis elegy: all these and the shifts of scene, tone, and viewpoint can suggest confusion rather than control. While none of the individual scenes is as puzzling to decipher as several of the episodes in *The Blue Mountains of China* and *The Temptations of Big Bear*, the problem of entering this expansive but confusing fictional world remains. My own first reading broke down in puzzlement as I tried to account for the apparently capricious shiftings of the spectral narrator. Only when I started again and read more carefully did the shape of the book ultimately reveal itself. The novel is best approached, I suspect, as a series of imaginative tableaux—what Falcon calls "'moments' that are telling you the essence of things" (194); and in this respect it proceeds like *The Blue Mountains of China*, through the cumulative effect of significant "spots of time."

The book lacks the gradual development to which we are accustomed in a traditional novel; instead, each section relates to the next not by any necessary plot-connection but because it adds yet another facet to our ultimate understanding of Riel. Frequently, these scenes explode ("explode," like "vision," is one of the keywords in the novel) into moments of extraordinarily moving visionary experience. Sometimes these are historical, like the account of Riel's vision in the cathedral at Washington in 1875, for which, Falcon assures us, he has "used Louis Riel's words" (140); others are Wiebe's invention, including the remarkable account of a sexual encounter between Riel and Marguerite, the kind of scene which Wiebe has not attempted before and which shows the astonishing emotional range that he can now encompass. Most impressive of all, in my opinion, is the scene in

Fort Benton church when Riel's intense and complex religious emotion spills over into Dumont's consciousness:

> And in that silence shivering still of hatred and mercy, Gabriel found his own rough voice. So strongly reduced from its usual size that he could not recognize it as his own, nor that the words moved farther than the strange, contra-dictory . . . saint? . . . he could not know for he had never met one, and the very notion rising in his head was like the words so strangely searching out something he had never prayed . . .

Together, conscious of the "wonder" reflected in each other's eyes, the two men go out to continue their journey,

> and beyond the horses and wagons and people patiently waiting for them they saw that hill again and in a glance knew they had both seen that revelation: a gallows there and a man swinging from that gallows. Vision and certainty. (188)

The vision and certainty are not merely asserted; they are recreated within a prose that modulates from the stuttering bewilderment of the prosaic Dumont caught up in an unprecedented moment of ecstasy to the serene presentation of the shared prophetic moment when both men recognize what lies ahead. "When you see that, you know." So ends both chapter and part, and the words sum up not only the revelation accorded to Riel and Dumont but the reader's response to Wiebe's art. I know of no other Canadian novelist—indeed, no other novelist—now writing who has attempted, let alone achieved, the heightened effect Wiebe produces here. After experiencing the full force of scenes like this, the reader recognizes himself in the presence of an unquestionably major novelist. When you see that, you know indeed.

7 Conclusion

I have concentrated in this study on Rudy Wiebe's novels, culminating in his achieved epic or "giant" fiction, because they are obviously the most important products of his creative work.[1] But he has also written a considerable number of short stories and has collaborated with Theatre Passe Muraille on the play *Far As the Eye Can See*; moreover, *The Mad Trapper*, a medium length novella, appeared just as this book was going to press. These deserve some attention here, all the more so since, like Frederick Philip Grove's short stories, they can generally be recognized as offshoots from the various clusters of interests and experiences that gave rise to the major fictions. A short account of these other writings will provide a convenient recapitulation since in them Wiebe's creative career can be traced in miniature.

His early stories of life—and, particularly, death—in isolated prairie communities clearly derive from the same biographical origins as *Peace Shall Destroy Many*. They include "Scrapbook" (his first published story which originally appeared under an inaccurate editorial title, "The Midnight Ride of an Alberta Boy," after winning first prize in a competition while Wiebe was still an undergraduate at the University of Alberta), "Tudor King" and an uncollected and less successful story, "The Power." At first reading, all seem straightforward from the formal or technical point of view, but on closer inspection they show signs of a conscious, if not always fully sustained, artistry. The small boys who act as central figures in the first two stories are virtually indistinguishable from each other and from Hal Wiens in the novel, and they clearly originate in Wiebe's own childhood experience. "Scrapbook" is ostensibly the story of an elder sister's premature death; since we know, to quote Patricia Morley, that "Wiebe first experienced death at the age of eight or nine when his seventeen-year-old sister died,"[2] we can reasonably assume that, in its essential feeling if not in the specific details, it reproduces authentic biographical material. But the interest of the story derives principally from Wiebe's success in recreating not so much the events themselves as the way in which they filter through a child's consciousness. Bud is sent off on horseback in the middle of the night to get help from the nearest neighbours, and although he understands the seriousness of the situation, he cannot help first seeing himself in terms of the stories with which he is familiar ("all by himself, just as he had read in *Black Beauty*" [*WV*, 16]), and then planning the exciting tale he will tell next day to his schoolfriends. At the same time, his own fear is projected on to the spruce and muskeg through which he rides, and these create the most powerful images in the whole story. The style catches the vivid directness of the child's responses—"Except for the dogs, he knew he could not have opened his mouth against the night" (*WV*, 16); "sleep kept pulling his head over as the house came closer" (*WV*, 17). The full impact of his sister's death only comes when he sees the school scrapbook which she had helped him to compile, and once again it comes in the child's terms: "He knew that 'dead' was like the sticks of rabbits he found in his snares" (*WV*, 18). Yet, though the viewpoint remains that of the child, we know that in a single night he has arrived upon the painful threshold of the adult world.

In "Tudor King," another small boy, Andy, has his illusions about Old Man Tudor's literal majesty shattered by his elder brother's scornful disbelief ("You've got to learn sometime that you can't believe everything" [*WV*, 22]). But, when they visit the old man after a five-day blizzard only to find him dead in his shack, and recognize his fruitless but under the circumstances heroic attempt to save his dog, Andy is able to retain (the phrase stressing a modified positive) a sense of "the fleeting stuff of human majesty" (*WV*, 25). Again the fact of death has to be faced and comprehended, and both stories end with the boys finding an emotional release in tears that they try not to shed. "Tudor King" is a successful if modest story in its own right, but for the student of Wiebe as a fictional craftsman its chief interest becomes manifest when he recognizes in the discovery of the body under the snow an early version of the climax at Brink Island in *First and Vital Candle*. None of the symbolic complexity exists in the short story, though the novel in turn loses some of the quality of moving simplicity that is achieved here. Together story and novel provide a fascinating instance of how a basic situation can develop so variously according to the tonal and intellectual requirements of different stories.

"All on Their Knees," written in the summer of 1964 though not published until 1968, is obviously a much more mature example of the story-maker's craft, and is more directly linked to *Peace Shall Destroy Many* since both novel and short story share one of the main characters as well as a common geographical locale. Herman Paetkau, the Mennonite ostracized for marrying a Métis woman in *Peace Shall Destroy Many*, is the central figure in the short story, and we find references to the Wapiti River, Poplar Lake, Hany (spelt "Hainy" in the novel), and the Métis Labret family. One veiled reference to Deacon Block and his daughter Elizabeth (*WV*, 76) depends for its meaning on a prior acquaintance with the novel, and we find here the kind of effect (never quite repeated by Wiebe) that is common in the work of William Faulkner, in which certain short stories add to our knowledge of characters in the novels and even alter our response to previous work.

This is a far more consciously crafted story than those we have hitherto considered. The title, with its reference to Hardy's poem "The Oxen," quoted later in the narrative, is indicative of a broader, "literary" concern. Herman's killing of the calf in order to feed the sick Indian, with its vague but suggestive allusion to the parable of the prodigal son, also communicates through literary reference, and the two are linked in the ending when Herman goes to the barn on Christmas night, with the legend recreated in Hardy's poem at the back of his mind, yet knowing all the time that he has already killed the calf that might otherwise have been on its knees.[3] Yet Herman's sacrifice of the calf for a fellow human being is part of an imaginative awakening of which his response to the poem is another symptom. And in a curious way his lie to the police on behalf of the Indian, his siding with the criminal against the law, creates a human and even (ironically) a Christian bond with the fugitive that becomes an enigmatic positive.[4] Wiebe is dealing with complex matters here, and the story can no longer be told with the straightforward directness of "Scrapbook." The opening sentences, like those of *First and Vital Candle* (see p. 36 above) plunge the reader powerfully if confusingly into the action: "Down on one knee he thrust his arms under, groping for a grip. It was curled, head and arms balled round to belly and knees. He fought the blizzard's weight and that unyielding curl, sweat bursting from his pores" (*WV*, 73). At first "he" and "it" are both equally mysterious; only gradually do we realize that "it" and the "curl" both refer to an unconscious body found in the snow. The immediate emphasis is on the struggle, a struggle we later understand as a heroic act, and the reader's initial sharing in this struggle helps to foster his sympathy with Herman and his actions later in the story.

Three of Wiebe's short stories, printed one after the other in *Where is the Voice Coming From?*, "Millstone for the Sun's Day," "There's a Muddy Road" and "Did Jesus Ever Laugh?," in some respects constitute new departures. We sense some radical experimentation at work here, as if Wiebe is earnestly—perhaps, even, rather desperately—trying to extend his fictional range. "Millstone for the Sun's Day" is set in an uncertain place and time, and works out, as Wiebe explained in a commentary when it was reprinted in John Metcalf's *The Narrative Voice*, the possible evolution of a literalist sect that based its practices on "some hard words spoken by the usually considerate Jesus" in the eighteenth chapter of St. Matthew's Gospel.[5] It is a brightly etched, compelling but chilling story that explores the familiar theme of violence within a religious community but in terms unrelated to anything else in Wiebe's work. One reviewer, J.R. (Tim) Struthers, claimed that it was "based on Shirley Jackson's story of ritualistic sacrifice entitled 'The Lottery'."[6] In fact, the emphases are very different, since "The Lottery," as its title implies, concentrates on the event itself whereas Wiebe is more interested in the theological perversion that could lead to such a practice; none the less, the connection is close enough to suggest that Wiebe may have been deliberately scrutinizing the work of other writers to test the extent to which he could transcend his Mennonite attitudes and relate to "modern" interests and subjects.

"Did Jesus Ever Laugh?," a first-person narrative reproducing the attitudes and thought-processes of a psychotic murderer, again juxtaposes religious belief (in this case, mania) with violence (in this case, sexual). One of Wiebe's most hauntingly memorable stories, it exists none the less in a contextual vacuum. Although Wiebe has elsewhere explored states that can be related, intellectually if not emotionally and psychologically, to that of the speaker—Abe Ross's frustrated attraction to the unnamed woman in *First and Vital Candle,* Jakob Friesen V's fall into sexual savagery in *The Blue Mountains of China,* the mentality of Albert Johnson, even perhaps Dumont's impulse to bloodthirsty revenge after Batoche—the story leads Wiebe outside the area in which he is naturally at ease. Similarly, "There's a Muddy Road," an indecisive account of a casual and unsuccessful affair, punctuated with images of mud and mess, explores a strand of life and subject-matter that we are familiar with in the fiction of such writers as Marian Engel and Richard B. Wright, but which seems far removed from Wiebe's interest or even knowledge. (And Struthers is surely right to see in the closing dialogue of this story an echo of the ending of D.H. Lawrence's *Women in Love.*[7]) These stories appear to have been written at a time when Wiebe was experimenting, conscious of his as yet undeveloped powers but uncertain of the next creative direction that they might take. They are often powerful and in themselves effective, but they seem to explore areas that (at least at the present stage in his development) have for Wiebe proved cul-de-sacs.

His more recent short stories have generally emerged from the same creative interests that produced *The Temptations of Big Bear* and *The Scorched-Wood People*. In many of them we find him experimenting with different and unfamiliar points of view. Allan Dueck has observed that Wiebe's stories and novels "have their bases in rural people with oral traditions—especially Mennonites and Indians—who have not distanced themselves from life by intellectualizing it."[8] As story-maker he is continually inventing or, perhaps more often, appropriating story-tellers. In "Along the Red Deer and the South Saskatchewan," for instance, a Blackfoot Indian (Little Bear) narrates to a white friend (F.W. Spicer) his story of a disastrous expedition against the Plains Cree. It is an epic-like story, and succeeds not only in establishing a heroic society ("that was our life, then" [*WV*, 123]) but in making the reader accept its mores and conventions. "The Fish Caught in the Battle River," on the other hand, employs a Scots narrator (in real life, Neil Brodie) who finds himself peripherally involved in the events surrounding Poundmaker and Riel in 1885. A reworked version of an authentic memoir, it moves backward and forward in time according to the whim of the speaker, and in so doing ironically throws the historical events into sharper relief. But whereas in "Along the Red Deer and the South Saskatchewan" the reader is invited by the sheer force of the storytelling to "think Indian," here the white narrator is shown developing a somewhat reluctant but none the less recognizable sense of respect for his Indian captors. The prejudice, the thinking in stereotypes which characterizes the opening of the story, has softened by its close. In Allan Dueck's words, "rather than mere enemies, the Indians have become people for Dan and the reader."[9]

Perhaps the most original and, for our purposes, rewarding stories are "Bluecoats on the Sacred Hill of the Wild Peas" and

"Where is the Voice Coming From?," since they explore not so much historical events themselves as the processes by which we come to understand historical events. I have examined the implications of the latter in chapters 1 and 5, so I will concentrate here on the "Bluecoats" story. It gives every indication of being based on Wiebe's own exploration of the site of "Custer's Last Stand," the area of the Little Big Horn in Montana where George Armstrong Custer and his men were destroyed in an unsuccessful attack on the Sioux in June 1876. The last sentence, in which the historian-father proposes driving "all the way home to Alberta" (*WV*, 111) suggests—and is obviously intended to suggest—the identification with Wiebe himself. The story depends for its effect on a constant juxtaposition of past and present. The historian, his wife, and three children are visiting the western United States in July 1969 at the time when the Americans are making their first landings on the surface of the moon. The visit also coincides with a Frontier Days festival at Cheyenne, Wyoming, and the story is punctuated by newspaper extracts reporting on the events. The ironies that can be extracted from such juxtapositions are legion. At the Frontier Days festival, the local Indians, descendants of those who defeated Custer, improvise a moon dance for the entertainment of the white tourists whose civilization has triumphed after all, not only in the old west but in the new frontier of outer space. Reference to "the huge sundance lodge" of 1876 (*WV*, 105) is followed by newspaper accounts of the ballroom of the Little America Motel where the moon landings are watched on specially-installed TV sets. The site of the battle itself has been altered and modernized; one of the historic spots has even been bulldozed flat, and elsewhere concrete paths mark the defence-lines. History has been adapted, and sacrificed, on behalf of the tourist trade. For the historian's small son, educated into the new mythology, Indians are inevitably associated with cowboys and the historical reality is difficult to understand; for the older girl, the horror of the killing—any killing—cuts across her response to the father's historical enthusiasm; for the wife, a campground with running water for bathing the baby takes precedence over all historic events, past or present.

There is little plot, merely an in-depth account of the visit. The effectiveness and artistry of the story lie in its total design, in the ironies, usually serious, painful ironies, that we register as we read. The father's efforts to reconstruct the events of a past time are set within a larger context, and it is characteristic of Wiebe's clear-headed honesty that the comparison is not always to the father's advantage. "Bluecoats on the Sacred Hill of the Wild Peas" is a historical reconstruction, a brooding on the ironies of history, and a humorous account of a family outing all in one, and for Wiebe the last is not necessarily the least important of the three. The immediately human is never undervalued. Just as "Where is the Voice Coming From?" becomes less a short story than a meditation on the methodology of history, so this story examines the ways in which historical events fit into the varied textures of our lives.

"Someday Soon, Before Tomorrow," an early story about the attempts of a collection of prairie farmers to resist the governmental bureaucracy that threatens their land and their livelihood, might almost have been written by Frederick Philip Grove. It takes as its centre the theme of man's relation to the land that we have seen as a constant preoccupation throughout Wiebe's as well as Grove's work. This is a subject which comes to the forefront again in *Far As the Eye Can See*, a play written by Wiebe in collaboration with actors from the Theatre Passe Muraille, a Toronto dramatic company. In the introduction to the printed text Wiebe describes the circumstances under which the play came into existence. After Wiebe had "developed the general concepts of place, subject and character" (*FES*, 6) with Paul Thompson, the artistic director of the theatre, four weeks of discussion, elaboration, and experiment were spent with the principal actors. Wiebe then wrote up the working script of the play (in eleven days), and it was further adapted during rehearsals for the first production in Edmonton (April 1977) and again prior to the second production in Toronto (December 1977). This background account is necessary because it indicates the elab-orateness of the collaboration at all stages in the growth of the play; it would probably be difficult for even Wiebe himself completely to disentangle his own original subject-matter and dialogue from the contributions of director and actors. We must therefore proceed with caution. None the less, by looking at the play within the context of his other work, it should be possible to recognize significant points of continuity.

Far As the Eye Can See was based on actual events connected with the Dodds-Round Hill Power Development Project near Edmonton between 1973 and 1976. Eighty farmers are threatened with the destruction of their land in the interests of a "Calgary Power" scheme to mine the coal that exists enticingly close to the surface. The most memorable character in the play, Anton Kalicz, believes (like the early Mennonite immigrants) in the rights guaranteed to the individual in Canada: "This is Canada, no Poland; here stand on your own land and you king" (*FES*, 26). The ironies implicit in this faith are explored throughout the play. Anton's son has become a successful Edmonton business-man more interested in the financial aspects of appropriation than in his father's links with the land, and his granddaughter, a college drop-out armed with all the rhetoric of radical protest, supports Anton for motives that are more emotionally sincere than intellectually well-founded.

But the play, as we might expect from the mature Wiebe, is firmly, and dramatically, set within the framework of history. The events of the 1970s are observed from above by a symbolic but lively trio representing "the Regal Dead": Crowfoot, the Indian chief who signed away his people's rights to the land in the 1870s; William Aberhart, Social Credit premier of Alberta in the last years of the Depression; and Princess Louise, from whom the province of Alberta, rather obscurely, derives its name. Their relations to Anton are complex. Crowfoot remarks: "I too was a king. Once" (*FES*, 15). Princess Louise, daughter of Queen Victoria and wife of a Governor-General, represents the British monarchy with which Crowfoot signed his treaty. Aberhart, the people's premier, with his championing of the little man against the financial interests of Toronto and New York, had originally inspired Anton to settle in Alberta in the first place. Yet, iron-ically, it is Aberhart, with his belief that "the resources of this province . . . will feed and clothe and shelter us" (*FES*, 16), who alone among the Regal Dead supports the development scheme. Indeed, one of the impressive features of *Far As the Eye Can See* is the careful balance maintained between the arguments for both sides. John Siemens, the engineer working for Calgary Power (and a Mennonite from Coaldale, where Wiebe lived during his adolescence), is no insensitive materialist, and his "dream" of the future (*FES*, 79), though far from the emotional centre of the play, is none the less powerful and carries weight. Although this is a play reflecting contemporary life, the emphasis on land and the attitudes towards it on the part of men and women from a wide variety of ethnic and social origins firmly links *Far As the Eye Can See* with the rest of Wiebe's creative work. In a recent interview, Wiebe observed: "What we need most, especially in drama, is material that comes out of our life here."[10] In this play he has begun the process of filling the need.

If the foregoing description suggests a sombre and didactic drama, a very different impression emerges from a stage perform-ance or even a sensitive reading of the printed text. One commen-tator, indeed, has described it as "a cheerful Irish stew of a play."[11] As might be expected in drama, "voice" becomes increasingly important here, and the linguistic range from Anton Kalicz's broken yet movingly eloquent English, through the prairie vernacular of the farmers, to the flattened, standardized speech of Anton's granddaughter is both well established and effectively blended. This helps to create the intensely human quality that pervades the play as a whole. Moreover, although at its heart this is a serious play on a serious subject, *Far As the Eye Can See* is full of exuberance and high spirits, and displays a wealth of comic and dramatic invention. Much of this may well belong to the per-formers' side of the collaboration. Thus the descent of Peter Lougheed, current premier of Alberta, as a political *deus ex machina* in an enormous coal-scoop—the stage direction dryly describes it as "too shiny and new ever to have been used yet"

(*FES*, 123)—is a theatrical *tour de force* hardly prepared for by anything that Wiebe has yet offered. Not the least exciting aspect of this collaboration is the possibility, indeed, likelihood, that the experience has assisted Wiebe in extending his own, already formidable creative range. The ramifications of this venture into the live theatre lie in the future, but it is a future we can look forward to with keen anticipation.

The work Wiebe has published since *The Scorched-Wood People* represents a period of consolidation and experiment. The short stories and sketches contributed to *Alberta/A Celebration* were produced for a specific occasion, the province's seventy-fifth birthday, and Wiebe was therefore under an obligation to represent the variety of Alberta's population and so go beyond the normal limits of his own range and interests. Connections with his earlier work are none the less frequent. In "Chinook Christmas" he draws for the first time on his teenage Mennonite experience at Coaldale; "The Funny Money of 1980" is narrated by William Aberhart whom he had just presented on stage in *Far As the Eye Can See;* and in "The Year We Gave Away the Land" Wiebe returns to the Indian treaties which gave the impetus to *The Temptations of Big Bear.* Other stories explore the industrial Alberta (which will eventually, one suspects, become the subject of a longer fiction), while "The Angel of the Tar Sands" is an intriguing experimental foray into the world of fantasy and magic realism.

The Mad Trapper, Wiebe's most recent published work at the time of writing, once more confronts the challenges of historical fact and imaginative interpretation. Here Wiebe returns to a subject he had explored briefly in a short story, "The Naming of Albert Johnson" (in *Where is the Voice Coming From?*), but now he seems less interested in probing the mystery of the material—Johnson's identity and the motives for his behaviour have never been fully established—than in creating through the medium of his art a historical pattern that the actual events seemed to lack.[12] Wiebe is far less concerned with historical fidelity here than in either *The Temptations of Big Bear* or *The*

Scorched-Wood People. In reality Albert Johnson shot Constable Edgar Millen on 29 January 1932. Wiebe substitutes an invented member of the RCMP on that occasion and has Millen confront Johnson on the banks of the Eagle River on 17 February where both fugitive and policeman die at the same time. Millen becomes obsessed with tracking down Johnson and, although the two began as moral and psychological opposites, as the fiction progresses they come to resemble each other more and more.

And Wiebe achieves this effect primarily through his art. Words and images associated with one man are gradually applied to the other. In the opening sections, Albert Johnson silently floating down river on his raft is juxtaposed with the noisy celebrations at Fort McPherson. There he briefly meets Millen for the first time and their paths separate until the fated and fatal encounter at the end of the book. This is Wiebe's most elaborately patterned book to date. At the same time, by introducing into his fiction newspaper reporters and radio operators who present Albert Johnson's story to the world in the clichés and conventions of the frontier-western, Wiebe distinguishes his own artistic concerns from the popular modes with which he is sometimes associated. What Wiebe communicates through his art is a fundamental integrity—a fidelity not to the facts of history but to the characters of men caught in the web of history. Even Albert Johnson, who remains a mystery and whose culpable actions are in no way condoned, emerges as a person of dignity, his ultimate privacy inviolate.

Clearly, a summing-up of Wiebe's literary achievement would be inappropriate at this time. Although he has already accomplished much, he is a writer decidedly in mid-career, and any descriptive assessment must inevitably be tentative. Moreover, while it is usually possible to classify a writer as either traditional or experimental, even this simple division breaks down in Wiebe's case. His traditional qualities are evident enough, but they are confined to the moral and religious positions which underpin his work. It would be a mistake to assume that he is traditional in the sense of conventional or unoriginal so far as the technical aspects of his work are concerned. On the contrary, as a "maker" he has always been excitingly inventive. Even *Peace Shall Destroy Many*, which began as a project in a creative writing course at the University of Alberta and shows him in the process of learning the basic skills of his craft, displays a distinctive use of technical effects, as my discussion in the second chapter aimed to demonstrate. But the advances since then have been enormous. *The Blue Mountains of China* dictates its own unique form, and the variety of effect in the novels of the north-west is truly astonishing. Indeed, the phrase that Coleridge used to describe *Antony and Cleopatra—feliciter audax*, happy valiancy—comes to mind as an appropriate term for the creative boldness that distinguishes his mature work. To take but one example, who but Wiebe would risk a comic interlude in the scene in *The Scorched-Wood People* between Riel's detention and his trial? Yet the presentation of the lawyers appointed to defend him, Lemieux, Fitzpatrick, and Greenshields, is a masterpiece of playful, undercutting irony. Indistinguishable from each other (as they must have seemed to Riel), they are presented as speaking, and even sighing, in unison (*SWP*, 318-321). The scene in no way detracts from the basic seriousness of the climax of Riel's story. Indeed, a sardonic sense of outrage comes through when we are told that, "confidently assisted by Lemieux, Fitzpatrick, and Greenshields, old Macdonald got his jury verdict: 'Guilty of high treason' " (*SWP*, 322); yet at the same time we respond with an exhilarated appreciation to the bubbling, irrepressible richness of Wiebe's art.

Stylistically, too, he has shown himself experimental and even daring. Unfortunately, the clotted heaviness of some of his earlier stylistic efforts caught the attention of reviewers, and the "clumsy writer" label has stuck fast. It is true that some decidedly rough edges can be found even in his recent work (one otherwise appreciative commentator has described him as "a writer whose tortured convolutions recall Faulkner's worst"[13]), and the effect is compounded by the number of misprints and errors that have managed to creep into his texts. In many respects, B. Pomer's allusion, as early as 1967, to his "hummocky prose style"[14] remains apt, but the resultant effect is by no means unsuccessful. In certain contexts, indeed, it proves invaluable. Robert Kroetsch has even gone so far as to praise Wiebe and Grove (among others) for their "marvellous ability to keep the language clumsy, brutal, unbeautiful, vital, charged."[15] An apt sinewy strength replaces the inappropriate euphonious elegance that is too often regarded as an artistic strength. Wiebe, Kroetsch argues, "is determined to destroy the sentence itself back to sense, back to its ground."[16]

Be that as it may, in concentrating more and more on the juxtaposition of voice and voice in his later fiction, Wiebe has slowly but surely achieved a greater variety and flexibility in his prose. Reviewers of *The Temptations of Big Bear*, in whatever way they responded, could not ignore the stylistic aspects of the book. Wiebe records that one "wanted to vomit"[17] but others found themselves referring to "its singing prose" and "a sensitive, carefully worked prose."[18] The point to be insisted on here is that Wiebe *uses* the stylistic resources of language in his fiction, whether in establishing speech patterns of individual characters (who, like the motorcyclist in *The Blue Mountains of China* or Thomas Scott in *The Scorched-Wood People*, are often judged by their employment of language) or in distinguishing between different views of the world (*e.g.*, the Indian/poetic, white/prosaic dichotomy in *The Temptations of Big Bear*). Here Wiebe differs in an interesting way from Frederick Philip Grove. Grove achieved most of his effects independently of the language he employed. His narrative prose communicates meaning but rarely contributes anything to the overall result. But when Wiebe creates one of his compelling and memorable scenes, the verbal rhetoric is responsible for a large part of its success. When, for example, Riel and Dumont see the gallows on the hill after leaving Fort Benton Church, the rhythm and urgency of the prose reinforce the significance of the scene, as I illustrated at the end of the previous chapter. We learn to listen to Wiebe's novels; sound and "voice" determine meaning. Dick Harrison has cogently pointed out that "more than most fiction or even most lyric, Wiebe's narration is overheard; it does not demand interpretation but rather patience, a suspension of judgments to wait for delayed significance."[19] Wiebe demands sympathetic perseverance on the part of his readers; ultimately, however, his prose yields up its secrets and, to adapt one of his own phrases, he can make the past sing in our ears with sweet songs (see *VL*, 138).

Wiebe is now firmly established as a novelist, yet his position within the exciting contemporary developments in Canadian literature is oddly ambiguous. He is very much a part of it, but remains enigmatically detached. Where, we may ask, is his voice coming from? Where does he fit? On the one hand he shows obvious suspicion of the ephemerally fashionable; when compiling *Stories from Western Canada* he observed: "One mark of authenticity in these stories . . . is that they do not pretend to trendiness."[20] On the other, even when his material is ostensibly historical he invariably manages to inject a modern note. Allan Bevan's comment on *The Temptations of Big Bear* is representative: "The novel is not only about the Indians of Western Canada at the end of their way of life; it is also about the continuing problems of all civilizations faced with inevitable changes, changes that force the destruction of the old values and the old codes of behavior."[21] Yet, and this point is often missed by his more superficial critics, when his work approaches either the "popular" or the contemporary, Wiebe raises the subject to his own level, transforms it for his own purpose, never lowers his standards to achieve an easy success. It is therefore important to challenge comments like the following, made by Heather Robertson in a popularizing article: "All Wiebe's themes are remarkably contemporary, even chic. His preoccupation with the macabre and the grotesque, his fascination with insanity, mysticism and revolution reflect the staple mythology of American pop culture. . . . *The Scorched-Wood People* is full of Good Guys and Bad Guys in a classic Western shoot-out," etc.[22] This kind of commentary is nothing less than irresponsible; not only is it inaccurate— Wiebe's interests do not "reflect" pop culture, and the novel in no way presents its characters in black-and-white stereotypes—but it can do harm by encouraging the simplification and vulgarization of serious literature. Insanity, mysticism, and revolution are age-old subjects that have interested writers from time immemorial. Superficial resemblances in subject-matter are ultimately of no account; the fact that both Shakespeare and Agatha Christie portray murderers leads to no connection between them. What matters is the quality of the work achieved, the validity of the imaginative world that the artist creates.

Wiebe has often been misrepresented in this way, even in the academic journals. Thus *First and Vital Candle* was criticized in the following terms by John Stedmond in the *University of Toronto Quarterly:* "Wiebe tries without marked success to mix adventure story *clichés* with sermonizing, presumably in order to render the latter more palatable."[23] The scene in Bjornesen's store is one that Stedmond evidently has in mind, and it assuredly contains many of the traditional ingredients of "Western" adventure: an upright hero attempting to rescue a girl kidnapped by seducers; a brawl; a deflected revolver shot; a last-minute twist to the plot, and so on. But Wiebe doesn't just employ the conventional features, he transforms them—restores them to something approaching their original and intrinsic force. He is aware of the popular stereotypes behind his subject, and even delights in creating a "serious" scene out of such hackneyed materials. In an earlier chapter I have discussed the allegorical framework on which this novel is based, and the "Western" associations of this particular scene belong to it. Similarly, the confrontations between Indians, Métis, and Mounties in *The Temptations of Big Bear* and *The Scorched-Wood People* derive, like the popular versions, from historical record, and Wiebe is able to present authentically and appropriately scenes that have too often been degraded by the "entertainment industry." The difference between the historian's reconstruction of "Custer's Last Stand" and his son's TV-oriented cowboy version in "Bluecoats on the Sacred Hill of the Wild Peas" is one of Wiebe's indirect but cogent commentaries on this whole problem; the contrast between the reporter's cliché-ridden version of the hunt for Albert Johnson and the dramatic situation that Wiebe presents in *The Mad Trapper* is another.

There are other ways in which Wiebe seems both contemporary and anti-contemporary. In a *Weltanschauung* committed to the anti-hero, he has persistently celebrated the heroic, not only the heroism of action but moral heroism as well. Yet this very heroism causes the unwary to associate his work with the clichés of popular culture. Again, when the dominant literary mood is best expressed in a self-deprecating, cynical irony, he has stressed uprightness and seriousness of purpose. Yet so various (perhaps muddled) are modern responses that resistance to one influential group inevitably suggests connections with another. Extremes tend to meet. Thus members of the radical protest-movements of the last two decades often display a moral earnestness and concern which recall Wiebe's even though he would find many of their attitudes and stances either petty or contemptible or both. Similarly, when limited aims are officially favoured, he has insisted on the need for "giant fiction." "It's very easy," he has remarked, "for us to write about the kinds of petty bedroom-bathroom problems that small people have" (*VL*, 154). He shows scant sympathy for "small people," whether those with modernistic pretensions (like Razia Tantamount in *Peace Shall Destroy Many*) or with excess money (like Irene Will[ia]ms in *The Blue Mountains of China*). But ordinary folk like Thom Wiens, or Abe Ross, or Frieda Friesen, or Anton Kalicz in *Far As the Eye Can See*, are portrayed with a sympathy that proves ennobling. In Wiebe the genuinely humble are exalted; if worthy, the little man is seen to be great. It is frivolity and the failure to aspire towards standards of behaviour which all human beings are capable of attaining that Wiebe finds unforgivable.

Above all, while Wiebe invariably writes about survival, which is a fashionable theme, he also writes about religious faith, which is not. There is no subject to which he has returned more consistently in interviews and public statements than his conviction about the supreme need at the present time—and, indeed, at all times—for faith and a set of moral and spiritual values. The following are samples only:

A religious faith, commitment, is absolutely essential in looking at the world.[24]

It seems to me that the religious and spiritual dimensions of the human being are of almost supreme importance in understanding the humanness of a character. That's not a given in most modern novels, especially in the post-Freudian novels. (*VL*, 166).

Throughout all ages, all the great writers have been committed to a spiritual and moral view of man and the universe. The morality of the world is built in. Man can't escape it. He can pretend he is free, but he is not.[25]

Such statements are likely to raise the hackles of the self-styled "liberated." Yet this same religious emphasis links him with a strong tradition in Canadian fiction that has continually found a fruitful subject-matter in the tensions between accepted beliefs (especially Puritan ones) and personal attitudes and actions. Moreover, Wiebe is religious in the Lawrentian as well as the Christian sense. That is to say, he is deeply, personally concerned with values that transcend the material, with the quality of human living. He writes less about faith itself than about the difficulties of faith and the human matrix out of which faith can be born. His books are novels, not tracts, because the emphasis is always on the individual rather than on the articles of faith in which he believes.

None the less, in the open, permissive literary milieu of the present time, when so many writers are fascinated, even obsessed, with subjects, attitudes, and language that have until recently been taboo, Wiebe is a somewhat anomalous figure. By eschewing an "anything goes" approach, and in keeping for the most part within traditional limits, he has been able to use the new freedoms sparingly but with particular effect when they suit his needs. Examples may be found in the language of the Russian guards in the "Cloister of the Lilies" section of *The Blue Mountains of*

China and the dramatically powerful use of the occasional four-letter word in *Far As the Eye Can See*. But Wiebe never flaunts these new freedoms, never allows them to obscure or besmirch his traditional moral stance. Once again, modern usages clothe orthodox and received standards. A curious moment in the interview between Eli Mandel and Wiebe in 1974 illustrates my point briefly but eloquently. After a wide-ranging and valuable discussion of Wiebe's work up to that time, Mandel suddenly asked, quite seriously, "Do you think that you've got a moral concern in your writing?" And Wiebe answered, with understandable surprise, "Yes, of course I do" (*VL*, 154). For Wiebe it could have been only a rhetorical question, but the fact that Mandel felt impelled to ask it at all indicates the cultural and intellectual distance that can separate Wiebe from his literary contemporaries and so, by implication, from many of his readers.

Wiebe's uneasy relations with his fellow writers is epitomised by his friendship with Robert Kroetsch. The two men obviously admire and respect each other, yet Kroetsch's literary interests and attitudes, and what it is now fashionable to call his life-style, are fundamentally opposed to Wiebe's. That Kroetsch's exuberant and iconoclastic cynicism catches a widespread posture of our time may be admitted, yet Wiebe's increasingly influential presence as a defender of traditional values should not be underestimated. Above all, the common interest of both men in the past of the land from which they sprang (in Kroetsch's case, the preoccupation suggested by the very title of *Gone Indian*, the implications behind the valley of dinosaur bones in *Badlands*, and the response to history embodied in *Stone-Hammer Poems*) suggests that, however far apart the two writers may seem, there are subtle links between them. Kroetsch has even gone so far as to describe Wiebe as "in some ways the most profoundly sexual of our writers."[26] At first this sounds paradoxical (one can imagine a playful glint in Kroetsch's eye as he wrote it) but there is a sense in which it is an extraordinarily cogent remark. In so far as Wiebe touches some of the deepest chords in the human psyche (the relation, for example, between Riel's sexuality and his religious vision), he is "profoundly sexual" at a time when most contemporary writers are only trivially so. Kroetsch reminds us that "modern" and "traditional" may not be quite such opposed labels as we sometimes assume. Certainly Wiebe's own position combines aspects of both.

His literary detachment is also evident in the numerous critical references to the work of his contemporaries scattered through his articles and his fiction (though against these should be set his generous praise of distinguished writing, especially Canadian, in the introductions to his anthologies). Perhaps the most conspicuous are Elizabeth Driediger's (and by implication, one suspects, Wiebe's) references to Stephen Vizinczey's *In Praise of Older Women* and Leonard Cohen's *Beautiful Losers* in *The Blue Mountains of China (BMC*, 182-3), and Razia Tantamount's enthusiasm for *The Sun Also Rises* (*PDM*, 169) which is obviously not shared by the narrator of *Peace Shall Destroy Many*. Others include criticism of Mary McCarthy, author of *The Group*, as one who "does not deserve to be mentioned in the same sentence" with William Faulkner,[27] and a sarcastic allusion in a recent article to "the bloody black Irish of Biddulph Township [who] are now recognizably the subject of (almost endless) high art" (*VL*, 211).

Such responses can easily be misinterpreted as self-centred and even arrogant. They are better explained, I think, as expressions of Wiebe's passionate conviction about the seriousness, and the sacredness, of his art. He recently acknowledged to Suzanne Zwarun that he is continually arguing with his fellow writers because "they have such incredible talent and they write about such terrible subjects."[28] The Puritan contempt for triviality here combines with the serious writer's undeviating commitment to the highest standards. "Words," he told Heather Robertson, "are too important for sheer entertainment,"[29] and the importance of a nation's story he believes to be even greater than that of words: "the stories we tell of our past are by no means merely words; they are meaning and life to us as *people*, as a *particular* people" (*VL*, 134). He has insisted that "the most original religious thinkers have also been great story-tellers"[30] (a remark that comes close to the heart of Wiebe's own artistic vision), and maintains that writers should always look upon their craft as a high calling with deep responsibilities. These observations are related to other statements about his own lofty ambitions, which can similarly be misconstrued. Heather Robertson quotes him as saying: "I want to be better than Nabokov, better than Faulkner, I want to write the greatest novel in North America,"[31] and she associates the remark with his interest in the ambitions of Riel. This is valid up to a point, but it needs to be balanced by an understanding of Wiebe's very real humility in relation to his art.[32] If one is going to be a writer, he implies, one must never offer less than one's best; no half-measures are acceptable. For Wiebe writing is a moral and religious act. He could say of his fiction what Dylan Thomas said of his poems, that they "are written for the love of Man and in praise of God, and I'd be a damn' fool if they weren't."[33] Excellence is demanded not in the interests of personal gratification but on behalf of man and God. It is therefore the duty as well as the "insatiable longing" of the committed writer "to once again write better than his best."[34] Out of this dedication Wiebe's "ambitious" statements arise.

His critics have generally been preoccupied with what they see as the excessive didacticism of Wiebe's work. Only at the present time, a literary historian might remark, would this emphasis seem unusual. The artist has traditionally been judged according to his capacity both to teach and to delight; the problem, as I have tried to indicate in my discussions of the individual novels, is not the fact of didacticism but Wiebe's success (or failure) in integrating his didactic impulses with the aesthetic requirements of his art. From *Peace Shall Destroy Many* to *The Scorched-Wood People* he has, I would argue, consistently refined and developed a necessary balance between these two elements. In the foreseeable future his critics, like Tolstoy's, will doubtless continue to argue about the artistic propriety of his moral emphases. Wiebe would, I believe, be content with this implicit association with the author of *Anna Karenina* and *War and Peace*. It is yet one more indication of the major if currently unfashionable tradition to which he belongs.

Wiebe can write giant or epic fiction because he believes in greatness and a hierarchy of standards. He has a low level of tolerance for writers who in his opinion do not live up to the highest demands of their art, and also for contemporary assertions about the equal suitability of all subject-matter. As he writes in his introduction to *The Story-Makers*, "some actions (and some professional activities!) can better show profound human depths than others."[35] So it is with characters in fiction. "I couldn't possibly write a novel," he told Brian Bergman, "about a character who didn't, to some extent at least, have a spiritual orientation towards the world and himself" (*VL*, 166). Although in his short stories he has explored the varied psychologies of the criminal, the psychotic, and the petty, he could never, like certain "moderns," put such characters at the centre of his work. And even these, figures like Albert Johnson or the spokesman of "Did Jesus Ever Laugh?" or even Almighty Voice (whom he has called "a petty human being" [*VL*, 154]) contain in their make up qualities worthy of artistic exploration. While discussing the literary mythology that has begun to grow around the character of Albert Johnson, "the mad trapper," Wiebe has written:

> What does it matter if, as seems likely the case, Johnson himself was really a nasty, misanthropic, vicious little man? I would find it impossible to write a novel about such a person, but in the last weeks of his life, when he with such single-minded violence labors to preserve his intact privacy, he does flame with a sheer human mystery.[36]

There is a whole theory of literary decorum beneath this statement, all the more valuable to us because it represents an attitude rarely heard at the present time.

The protagonists in Wiebe's novels must be worthy of their position, though they are never tiresome prototypes of impeccable virtue. However much he may sympathize with Big Bear and Louis Riel, he knows that their personalities can be interpreted less positively, and his invented characters like Thom Wiens, Abe Ross, and Jakob Friesen IV must all come to terms with their imperfections. But the "sheer human mystery" that Wiebe detects even in the actions of Albert Johnson is always present, and the extent to which it is present determines the attention which the character in question can bear. In a world constantly subjected to violence, Wiebe insists on the ongoing search for peace that invariably accompanies it (even in the unlikely guise of Albert Johnson's quest for "his intact privacy"). In this lies Wiebe's hope, and to it his work as a novelist is dedicated. His position is best summed up, perhaps, in a simple statement made to Eli Mandel: "I do believe in human greatness, and I do believe that at our best moments we should explore it" (*VL*, 154). For Wiebe himself, all moments when he is engaged in writing must be his best.

And what of the future? Here, of course, literary criticism either lapses into silence or gives way to the more dangerous art of prophecy. At the time at which I write (early in 1981) his completed work offers both shape and coherence. Development could occur in various directions. His most recent productions suggest no firm commitment. The artistic success of *Far As the Eye Can See* might well encourage him to pursue his newly-revealed dramatic talent, though it is difficult to believe that fiction will not continue to be his main form of creative expression. "Home for Night," a short story contributed to the *NeWest Review* (April 1976), with its presentation of the son of Mennonite pioneers returning guiltily and painfully to his birthplace on the death of his father, suggests a parallel return on Wiebe's part to contemporary and personal themes, and he admitted in a recent interview "that he needs a rest from the period of the rebellions."[37] On the other hand, he told Suzanne Zwarun that "he figures on mining the 1870s for two more prairie novels,"[38] and "In the Beaver Hills," which represents Wiebe in *Aurora: New Canadian Writing 1978*, is a confident and effective account of incidents in the life of the Cree chief Broken Arm that elaborate on certain passages in *The Temptations of Big Bear* and could form part, ultimately, of another full-length chronicle of Indian life. Half way between these extremes, "After Thirty Years of Marriage" (in *Alberta/A Celebration*) is a documentary chronicle of homesteading in the early years of the century that superficially harks back to Grove though its implications (the family is American, and most of them return home when they have got what they wanted) is chillingly contemporary; a rich balance is achieved between sympathy and judgement. *The Mad Trapper* is still based on history, but it is set much closer to our own time. The omens, therefore, may be indecisive but they are undoubtedly positive. Rudy Wiebe may well be poised for an exciting artistic advance. Whether this involves an unexpected change of direction remains to be seen, but, given the organic growth that has characterized his work so far, we can be sure that the seeds of his subsequent writings will germinate from the novels and short stories we already know. We can be sure, too, that Wiebe has a limitless supply of material for more epic fiction. A remark he made to Brian Bergman provides impressive evidence of his continuing creativity: "I'm hounded by a posse of possible stories to tell; I'll never be able to tell them all" (*VL*, 169).

Notes

1 Introduction

1. Wiebe has himself discussed this passage and its implications in "New Land, Ancient Land," in Richard Chadbourne and Hallvard Dahlie, eds., *The New Land: Studies in a Literary Theme* (Waterloo: Wilfrid Laurier University Press [for the Calgary Institute for the Humanities], 1978), pp. 2-3.

2. "Passage by Land," in John Metcalf, ed., *The Narrative Voice* (Toronto: McGraw-Hill Ryerson, 1972), p. 257. For an account of the area in which Wiebe spent his early years, see his "Tombstone Community" (*VL*, 16-24).

3. "Western Canadian Fiction; Past and Future," *Western American Literature*, 6 (Spring 1971), 27.

4. *Ibid.*, 24.

5. Wallace Stegner, *Wolf Willow: A History, a Story, and a Memory of the Last Plains Frontier* (1955; rpt. New York: Viking, 1958), p. 112.

6. "Passage by Land," pp. 257-58. For comparable remarks, see *VL*, 133-34, 217.

7. Stegner, p. 112.

8. E.K. Francis, *In Search of Utopia: The Mennonites in Manitoba* (Altona, Manitoba: D.W. Friesen, 1955), p. 5. This is probably the most convenient source for Mennonite beliefs and practices. For a briefer but useful account, see Gerhard Lohrenz's pamphlet, *The Mennonites of Western Canada* (Steinbach, Manitoba: Derksen Printers, 1974). For a more comprehensive historical survey, see Cornelius J. Dyck, ed., *An Introduction to Mennonite History: A popular history of the Anabaptists and the Mennonites* (Scottdale, Pennsylvania: Herald Press, 1967).

9. Donald Cameron, *Conversations with Canadian Novelists, Part Two* (Toronto: Macmillan, 1973), pp. 156-57. Wiebe discusses this matter in greater detail in "The Artist as a Critic and a Witness" (*VL*, 41-5).

10. For informative accounts of the political history of this emigration (helpful also as background to the "Black Vulture" chapter of *The Blue Mountains of China*), see Frank H. Epp, *Mennonite Exodus* (Altona, Manitoba: D.W. Friesen, 1962) and Harvey L. Dyck, "Collectivization, Depression, and Immigration, 1929-1930: A Chance Interplay," in Harvey L. Dyck and H. Peter Krosby, eds., *Empire and Nations: Essays in Honour of Frederic H. Soward* (Toronto: University of Toronto Press in association with the University of British Columbia, 1969), pp. 144-59.

11. Wiebe offers a brief summary of these origins in "The Meaning of Being Mennonite Brethren" (*VL*, 32-3). For a more detailed account, see Frank C. Peters and Cornelius J. Dyck, "The Mennonite Brethren Church," chapter 15 of Cornelius J. Dyck, ed., *An Introduction to Mennonite History*.

12. Francis, pp. 262-63.

13. See Heather Robertson, "Western Mystic," *Canadian Magazine* [*Toronto Star*] (10 December 1977), 22.

14. See George Melnyk, "Rudy Wiebe and other rebels," *Quill and Quire*, 43 (November 1977), 31.

15. Cameron, p. 148.

16. "Passage by Land," p. 259. It is interesting to note that Wiebe praised Grove for presenting "the *giant* hard world of the pioneer farmer" (my italics) in "Western Canadian Fiction; Past and Future," 27.

17. Introduction to *The Story-Makers* (Toronto: Macmillan, 1970), p. xiv.

18. Cameron, p. 152. Cf.: "The old distinction between fiction and life as it is lived has broken down completely. The TV documentary has done a lot of this. I see great possibilities for this." Margaret Reimer and Sue Steiner, "Translating life into art: A conversation with Rudy Wiebe" (*VL*, 129-30).

19. "New Land, Ancient Land," p. 4.

20. This linguistic concern is also central to the novel by virtue of the fact that language has always been regarded as crucial to the survival of the Mennonites as a people. *The Blue Mountains of China* is full of minor effects dependent on language (the conversation in "On the Way," for instance, much of which is supposed to take place in Low German) that a non-Mennonite reader is unlikely to pick up. I am indebted to my colleague, Magdalene Redekop, for deepening my awareness of this aspect of Wiebe's art. See also her illuminating essay, "Translated into the Past: Language in *The Blue Mountains of China*" (*VL*, 97-123).

21. This photograph is reproduced with the text of Wiebe's story in Ken Mitchell, ed., *Horizon: Writings of the Canadian Prairie* (Toronto: Oxford University Press, 1977), p. 40. It may also be found in George Woodcock, *Faces from History: Canadian Profiles and Portraits* (Edmonton: Hurtig, 1978), p. 139.

22. Cf.: "For nearly a month now every Cree had sounded the same to the Governor. He had found it best to concentrate completely on Peter Erasmus' words, but now he found his head turning into blackness, slowly down into the

enormous, strange depths of that incomprehensible voice" (*TBB*, 19).

23. "Passage by Land," p. 260.

24. Wiebe makes this point himself in Brian Bergman's interview, "Rudy Wiebe: Storymaker of the Prairies" (*VL*, 167-68).

2   *Peace Shall Destroy Many*

1. E.K. Francis, *In Search of Utopia: The Mennonites in Manitoba* (Altona, Manitoba: D.W. Friesen, 1955), p. 78.

2. Allan Dueck, "Rudy Wiebe as Storyteller: Vision and Art in Wiebe's Fiction" (Unpublished M.A. thesis, University of Alberta, 1974), p. 49.

3. For evidence that Block's attitude to "the breeds" was shared by many of the original Mennonite settlers, see Francis, pp. 41, 42.

4. Patricia A. Morley, *The Comedians: Hugh Hood and Rudy Wiebe* (Toronto: Clarke Irwin, 1977), p. 71.

5. On Grove's novelistic artistry, see my "The Art of Frederick Philip Grove: *Settlers of the Marsh* as an Example," *Journal of Canadian Studies,* 9 (August 1974), 26-36.

6. Many of Wiebe's editorials in the *Mennonite Brethren Herald,* written about the time *Peace Shall Destroy Many* was published, reflect a comparable testing of position in his church activities. These include "Evaluative Criticism: An Essential in the Church" (27 April 1962), "Conscription for Military Service" (11 May 1962), "Foreign Missions across the Street" (26 October 1962) and, looking forward to *The Blue Mountains of China,* "Why Bother with Mennonite History?" (23 November 1962).

7. Peter Klassen, "Mennonites and Culture: The Saengerfest," in William De Fehr, ed. *Harvest: Anthology of Mennonite Writing in Canada* (Centennial Committee of the Mennonite Historical Society of Manitoba, 1974), p. 34; Francis, p. 270; "The Death and Life of Albert Johnson: Collected Notes on a Possible Legend," in Diane Bessai and David Jackel, eds., *Figures in a Ground: Canadian Essays on Modern Literature Collected in Honor of Sheila Watson* (Saskatoon: Western Producer Prairie Books, 1978), p. 219.

8. Donald Cameron, *Conversations with Canadian Novelists, Part Two* (Toronto: Macmillan, 1973), p. 155. Cf.: "That Christmas of 1962 was quite a convulsion. . . . the book was the only topic of conversation at the dinner table because it was the first realistic novel about Mennonites ever written in English." Wiebe quoted in George Melnyk, "Rudy Wiebe and other rebels," *Quill and Quire,* 43 (November 1977), 31. Wiebe's editorial, "A Personal Word to Friends" (*Mennonite Brethren Herald* [21 June 1963]), is a dignified and moving statement of his position at that time which clearly reveals tensions beneath the surface. Obviously, the *Peace Shall Destroy Many* controversy only brought to a head disagreements which had been festering for some time. For an account of

the Mennonite reviews of *Peace Shall Destroy Many*, and a reprinting of Herbert Giesbrecht's review in the *Canadian Mennonite* and Wiebe's reply, see *VL*, 50-63.

9. Heather Robertson, "Western Mystic," *Canadian Magazine* [*Toronto Star*] (10 December 1977), 22.

10. This point is argued at length in Elmer F. Suderman, "Universal Values in *Peace Shall Destroy Many*" (*VL*, 71-2).

3   *First and Vital Candle*

1. See, for example, Jim Christy, "A Personal Christianity," *Saturday Night*, 86 (28 April 1971), 28, and B. Pomer, *Canadian Forum*, 47 (January 1968), 236. In the latter case, however, the reviewer makes the distinction between subject-matter and novelistic form.

2. Wiebe has clearly been influenced in his presentation of Abe Ross by the career of Duncan Pryde, whose memoir of his years in the Arctic, *Nunaga: My Land, My Country* (Edmonton: Hurtig) appeared in 1971. Wiebe wrote a review of the book ("Guys Who Stay Out in the Cold," *Books in Canada*, 1 [December 1971], 7-8), and records there that he first met Pryde in July 1964. He describes him, in words that recall Ross, as "a Scottish orphan in the grand tradition of the Hudson's Bay Company trading for furs on the Barren Grounds" (8). Allan Dueck observes that the section concerning Oolulik "grew out of a story that Duncan Pryde told Wiebe about his Arctic experiences" ("Rudy Wiebe as Storyteller: Vision and Art in Wiebe's Fiction" [Unpublished M.A. thesis: University of Alberta, 1974], p. 7). Wiebe also seems to have adapted some of Pryde's Eskimo experiences in creating his Indian community of Frozen Lake. The replacing of an unsatisfactory trader, the degradation of the trappers and their families through homebrew, and certain details of Ross's efforts to remedy the situation all find parallels in Pryde's subsequently published *Nunaga*. Wiebe even appropriates Pryde's surname and gives it to another trader in the area (see *FVC*, 99-100).

3. The quoted phrase is John Stedmond's, in a review of a collection of essays including "Passage by Land" in *University of Toronto Quarterly*, 43 (Summer 1974), 411.

4. S.E. Read, "Maverick Novelist," *Canadian Literature*, no 31 (Winter 1967), 77.

5. It is interesting to note Wiebe's later, much more complicated use of this effect in the backward-moving time-structure of the short story, "The Naming of Albert Johnson," in *Where is the Voice Coming From?*.

6. Patricia A. Morley, *The Comedians, Hugh Hood and Rudy Wiebe* (Toronto: Clarke Irwin, 1977), p. 95n.

7. *Ibid.*, p. 86.

8. As a note in the Wiebe papers at the University of Calgary indicates, his source for these details was A. Irving Hallowell's *The Rise of Conjuring in Saulteaux Society* (Philadelphia: University of Pennsylvania Press, 1942). In this monograph Hallowell observes that "cases are reported in which lost articles have been tossed out of the conjuring tent to their owners" and cites one instance in which a man "had just come up the river and had lost his gun in the water. The old conjurer had a lodge erected and sent one of his *pawáganak* [spirits] for the gun. He then handed it out to the man who had lost it" (pp. 68, 69).

9. Morley, p. 88.

4   *The Blue Mountains of China*

1. See Heather Robertson, "Western Mystic," *Canadian Magazine* [Toronto *Star*] (10 December 1977), 20.

2. R.P. Bilan, "Wiebe and Religious Struggle," *Canadian Literature*, no 77 (Summer 1978), 58. Moreover, as Magdalene Redekop has pointed out to me, David Epp's going back may be seen as symbolically contrasted to John Reimer's going forward in the chapter entitled "On the Way."

3. It is worth noting at this point that the chapter "Wash, This Sand and Ashes" is based on an incident from Wiebe's own experience which he described at the time as follows: "On October 30 [1966] when I drove north into Moro country with Rolf Fostervold, New Tribes worker stationed in Filadelphia, we met a Moro with a cactus spina in his foot. The foot was hugely swollen and filled with pus. We did not get to Cero Leon as we intended; we had to bring this man, Osowané, to the Fernheim doctor." "Moros and Mennonites in the Chaco of Paraguay" (*VL*, 85).

4. Cf.: "I get bored with people raking over their own viscera." Wiebe quoted in George Melnyk, "Rudy Wiebe and other rebels," *Quill and Quire*, 43 (November 1977), 31.

5. Lord David Cecil, *Hardy the Novelist* [1943] (London: Constable, 1960), p. 140.

6. D.W. Doerksen, "Looking for a Place to Call Their Own," *Mennonite Brethren Herald* (22 January 1971), 22.

7. Bilan, 63. For another stimulating discussion of the ending of the novel, approaching similar conclusions to my own by a rather different route, see David L. Jeffrey, "A Search for Peace: Prophecy and Parable in the Fiction of Rudy Wiebe" (*VL*, 190-93).

8. Doerksen, 22.

9. I am indebted to Magdalene Redekop for help in formulating my position here.

10. Donald Cameron, *Conversations with Canadian Novelists, Part Two* (Toronto: Macmillan, 1973), pp. 149-50.

5   *The Temptations of Big Bear*

1. "Western Canadian Fiction; Past and Future," *Western American Literature*, 6 (Spring 1971), 29.

2. Cf. Wiebe's remark to Marsha Erb: "Big Bear had a good mind and was one of the greatest men this country has ever seen." "An author's view of his homeland," *Saskatoon Star-Phoenix* (2 November 1973).

3. See Ray Chatelin, "Tragic Story of Big Bear," *Vancouver Province* (4 December 1973).

4. See Allan Dueck, "Rudy Wiebe as Storyteller: Vision and Art in Wiebe's Fiction." Unpublished M.A. thesis (University of Alberta, 1974), p. 7.

5. Donald Cameron, *Conversations with Canadian Novelists, Part Two* (Toronto: Macmillan, 1973), p. 150. In the first edition of *The Temptations of Big Bear*, a prefatory statement by Wiebe was printed with the introductory material. Since it is similarly concerned with the historical authenticity of the characters and is not included in the New Canadian Library reprint, I reproduce it here: "No name of any person, place or thing, insofar as names are still discoverable, in this novel has been invented. Despite that, and despite the historicity of dates and events, all characters in this meditation upon the past are the products of a particular imagination; their resemblance and relation, therefore, to living or once living persons is to be resisted."

6. John Wilson Croker, review of *Waverley* in the *Quarterly Review*, quoted in John Lauber, *Sir Walter Scott* (New York: Twayne, 1966), p. 50.

7. Cameron, p. 150.

8. Introduction to *The Story-Makers* (Toronto: Macmillan, 1970), p. xxv.

9. Cameron, pp. 158-59.

10. "New Land, Ancient Land," in Richard Chadbourne and Hallvard Dahlie, eds., *The New Land: Studies in a Literary Theme* (Waterloo: Wilfrid Laurier University Press [for the Calgary Institute for the Humanities], 1978), p. 3.

11. John Moss, *Sex and Violence in the Canadian Novel: The Ancestral Present* (Toronto: McClelland and Stewart, 1977), p. 269.

12. Ken Adachi, "Unusual author lives a life of Canadian example," *Toronto Star* (4 November 1977).

13. Frank Davey, *From There to Here* (Erin, Ontario: Press Porcepic, 1974), p. 267.

14. Robert Kroetsch and Diane Bessai, "Death is a Happy Ending: A Dialogue in Thirteen Parts," in Diane Bessai and David Jackel, eds., *Figures in a Ground: Canadian Essays on Modern Literature Collected in Honor of Sheila*

Watson (Saskatoon: Western Producer Prairie Books, 1978), p. 213.

15. David Williams in *Queen's Quarterly*, 81 (Spring 1974), 143. However, Wiebe once maintained in an interview, "in answer to a question, that he was not—at least not consciously—finding in the Indians a metaphor for his own experience, as the member of another minority culture, the Mennonites." Alan Dawe, "Untaped Interviews," *Event*, 4 (1974), 36.

16. Cf.: "The names of the police sound very much alike; they all begin with Constable or Corporal or Sergeant . . . " (*WV*, 136).

17. See R.P. Bilan, "Wiebe and Religious Struggle," *Canadian Literature*, no 77 (Summer 1978), 52.

18. "The Year of the Indian," *Dalhousie Review*, 54 (Spring 1974), 166.

6   *The Scorched-Wood People*

1. Donald Cameron, *Conversations with Canadian Novelists, Part Two* (Toronto: Macmillan, 1972), p. 150.

2. Wiebe makes no more pretence at objectivity in this novel than in *The Temptations of Big Bear*. He told one interviewer: "You bet I'm biased about Riel, and I don't try to hide it." George Jacub, "Louis Riel visionary, not madman: Wiebe," *Winnipeg Tribune* (4 November 1977).

3. Peter Charlebois, *The Life of Louis Riel* (Toronto: NC Press, 1975), p. 101.

4. "The Year of the Indian," *Dalhousie Review*, 54 (Spring 1974), 165.

5. Bernard de Voto, Introduction to Joseph Kinsey Howard, *Strange Empire: A Narrative of the Northwest* (New York: Morrow, 1952), p. 9.

6. Georg Lukács, *The Historical Novel*. Translated from the German by Hannah and Stanley Mitchell [1962] (Harmondsworth: Penguin Books, 1969), p. 303.

7. George Woodcock, "Riel and Dumont," *Canadian Literature*, 77 (Summer 1978), 99.

8. Lukács, pp. 15, 52, 57, 193.

9. *Ibid.*, p. 303.

10. Woodcock, "Riel and Dumont," 99.

11. George Woodcock, *Gabriel Dumont: The Métis Chief and his Lost World* (Edmonton: Hurtig, 1975), p. 7.

12. Woodcock, "Riel and Dumont," 100. It is interesting to note that other reviewers responded much more positively to Dumont. Thus Ken Adachi, in the *Toronto Star* (29 October 1977), described him as "a man of enormous appeal, loving, kind, generous, and a paradigm of all that was vital in the Métis"; and R.P. Bilan, in the *University of Toronto Quarterly* (47 [Summer 1978] 337), found the Dumont of *The Scorched-Wood People* "a warm and appealing figure."

13. Wiebe is recorded as saying: "I remember a conversation in which Mel Hurtig tried to convince me how magnificent Dumont was, and I said he was just a bloodthirsty cut-throat. But I've grown to like him a lot better now." Quoted in George Melnyk, "Rudy Wiebe and other rebels," *Quill and Quire*, 43 (November 1977), 31. An additional problem here, which I gladly leave to the historians, stems from the possibility that Woodcock's gentle anarchist may be as subjective a portrait of Dumont as Wiebe's tough man of action.

14. Lukács, p. 48.

15. *Ibid.*, p. 35.

16. "Western Canadian Fiction; Past and Future," *Western American Literature*, 6 (Spring 1971), 25.

17. One reviewer argued that "when we embark on the story of Riel, Dumont, the Bois-Brûlés, I imagine us like people in Athens entering the Theatre of Dionysus to witness the story of Agamemnon, or Oedipus, or Hippolytus, a story whose broad outlines and tragic finale we already know." Don Kerr, "Like Any Thunderstorm," *NeWest Review*, 3 (February 1978), 3. Doubtless the dramatic quality of the novel also derives from the fact that the CBC originally invited Wiebe to write a series of television plays on Riel and the Métis. A victim of budget-cuts, the production was severely modified and delayed, and Wiebe dropped out of the project. For Wiebe's interest in the cinematographic elements in Riel's story, see "Riel: A Possible Film Treatment" (*VL*, 158-62).

18. Melnyk, "Rudy Wiebe and other rebels," 31.

19. Woodcock, "Riel and Dumont," 99.

20. Dick Harrison, "Cultural Insanity and Prairie Fiction," in Diane Bessai and David Jackel, eds., *Figures in a Ground: Canadian Essays on Modern Literature Collected in Honor of Sheila Watson* (Saskatoon: Western Producer Prairie Books, 1978), p. 292.

21. See *ibid.*, pp. 292, 293.

22. "The Death and Life of Albert Johnson; Collected Notes on a Possible Legend," in Bessai and Jackel, p. 239.

23. This, incidentally, is an authentic Falcon ballad. Both text and translation can be found in *White Pelican*, 1 (Summer 1971), 22-5, or in N. Brian Davis, ed. *The Poetry of the Canadian People, 1720-1920* (Toronto: NC Press, 1976), pp. 248-52.

24. Wallace Stegner, *Wolf Willow; A History, a Story, and a Memory of the Last Plains Frontier* (1955; rpt. New York: Viking, 1958), p. 112.

25. Falcon's position as an orthodox though undogmatic Catholic is also, of course, important here. Once again he acts as mediator. While sharing many of Riel's religious attitudes, he does not follow him in his extreme dismissal of the authority of Rome. Similarly, his Christianity (though very different from Wiebe's) allows him to share with the novelist a Christian approach to history, a sense of meaning within historical process.

26. Compare the anecdote on p. 175 of the novel with "A Novelist's Personal Notes on Frederick Philip Grove" (*VL*, 215-16).

7 Conclusion

1. Some literary commentators may still dispute this judgment. As late as 1975, Donald Stephens wrote in a review of *Where is the Voice Coming From?*: "Wiebe is much better with the short story, as a form, than he is with the novel" ("A World Sequestered," *Canadian Literature*, no. 63 [Winter 1975], 102). It seems to me, however, that this view becomes less and less tenable as Wiebe's career as a novelist develops.

2. Patricia A. Morley, *The Comedians: Hugh Hood and Rudy Wiebe* (Toronto: Clarke Irwin, 1977), p. 13.

3. This applies to the story as it appears in *Where is the Voice Coming From?* The version published in *The Mennonite* contained an additional paragraph in which Herman is killed by the Indian when, on entering the barn, he finds him in the act of stealing a horse.

4. In "Reader engaged in dialogue with darkness," a review in the *London Free Press* (1 February 1975), J.R. (Tim) Struthers argued that the story was modelled on Albert Camus' "The Guest," which Wiebe printed in translation in *The Story-Makers*. But although there are admittedly certain superficial plot-resemblances, Camus' story concentrates characteristically on an existential dilemma while Wiebe's focuses on the moral action of a human being and its effect on his consciousness. As Wiebe himself remarked in another context, "I write as a Christian just as Camus writes as an existentialist." Margaret Reimer and Sue Steiner, "Translating life into art: A conversation with Rudy Wiebe" (*VL*, 127).

5. John Metcalf, ed., *The Narrative Voice* (Toronto: McGraw-Hill Ryerson, 1972), p. 259.

6. For Struthers, see note 4 above. "The Lottery" originally appeared in the *New Yorker* and was collected in *The Lottery* (New York: Farrar, Straus, 1949).

7. For Struthers, see note 4 above.

8. Allan Dueck, "Rudy Wiebe as Storyteller: Vision and Art in Wiebe's Fiction" (Unpublished M.A. thesis: University of Alberta, 1974), p. 3.

9. *Ibid.*, p. 79. Wiebe draws heavily for the first story on F.W. Spicer's account of Little Bear's personal narrative first published by John Hawkes in *The Story of Saskatchewan and Its People* (3 vols. Chicago-Regina: S.J. Clarke Publishing Company, 1924), I, 109-23. "The Fish Caught in the Battle River" is based upon a pamphlet by Neil Brodie, *Twelve Days with the Indians* (Battleford: Saskatchewan Herald, 1932). For a study of the relations between these stories and their sources, see my "From Document to Art: Wiebe's Historical Short Stories and Their Sources," *Studies in Canadian Literature*, 4 (Summer 1979), 106-19.

10. George Melnyk, "Rudy Wiebe and other rebels," *Quill and Quire*, 43 (November 1977), 31.

11. Alexander Leggatt, "Drama," *University of Toronto Quarterly*, 47 (Summer 1978), 374.

12. Wiebe's main source for the historical details in *The Mad Trapper* is Dick North, *The Mad Trapper of Rat River* (Toronto: Macmillan, 1972).

13. Wayne Tefs, "Rudy Wiebe: Mystery and Reality," *Mosaic*, XI/4 (Summer 1978), 155.

14. B. Pomer, review of *First and Vital Candle*, *Canadian Forum*, 47 (January 1968), 235.

15. Robert Kroetsch, "Unhiding the Hidden: Recent Canadian Fiction," *Journal of Canadian Studies*, 3, no 3 (1974), 45.

16. *Ibid.*

17. Heather Robertson, "Western Mystic," *Canadian Magazine* [*Toronto Star*] (10 December 1977), 20. The reference is to David Watmough in a CBC broadcast.

18. David Williams, *Queen's Quarterly*, 81 (Spring 1974), 142; Laurence Ricou, *University of Windsor Review*, 10 (Spring-Summer 1975), 81.

19. Dick Harrison, *Unnamed Country: The Struggle for a Canadian Prairie Fiction* (Edmonton: University of Alberta Press, 1977), p. 202.

20. Introduction, *Stories from Western Canada* (Toronto: Macmillan, 1972), p. xi.

21. Allan Bevan, Introduction, *The Temptations of Big Bear* (New Canadian Library. Toronto: McClelland and Stewart, 1976), p. xiii.

22. Robertson, 22.

23. John Stedmond, "Fiction," *University of Toronto Quarterly*, 36 (Summer 1967), 386.

24. Quoted (from a CBC tape) in Morley, p. 121.

25. Suzanne Zwarun, "Lonely are the grave," *Maclean's*, 91 (4 September 1978), 37.

26. Robert Kroetsch, "Mirror, mirror show us all" [review of *The Scorched-Wood People*], *Books in Canada*, 7 (January 1978), 14.

27. "Western Canadian Fiction; Past and Future," *Western American Literature*, 6 (Spring 1971), 22.

28. Zwarun, 34.

29. Robertson, 22.

30. Introduction, *Double Vision* (Toronto: Macmillan, 1976), p. xii.

31. Robertson, 22.

32. One of the few commentators to notice this humility is F.G. Martinson: "Rudy is a quiet, easy-going fellow who speaks humbly of himself and his work, a quality rapidly disappearing among writers and critics." "Meet Rudy Wiebe," *Canadian Review*, 1 (April 1974), 9.

33. Dylan Thomas, "Note" to *Collected Poems 1934-1952* (London: Dent, 1952), p. vii.

34. Introduction, *Double Vision*, p. xii.

35. Introduction, *The Story-Makers* (Toronto: Macmillan, 1970), p. xxvii.

36. "The Death and Life of Albert Johnson: Collected Notes on a Possible Legend," in Diane Bessai and David Jackel, eds., *Figures in a Ground: Canadian Essays on Modern Literature Collected in Honor of Sheila Watson* (Saskatoon: Western Producer Prairie Books, 1978), p. 246. The recently published *Mad Trapper* seems to contradict this statement, but the contradiction is, I believe, superficial. Wiebe's building up of the character of Edgar Millen until he becomes Johnson's moral shadow is Wiebe's answer to this problem. Johnson is not a central dominating figure in the way that Big Bear and Riel had been. The centre of this novella is not so much Johnson himself as "sheer human mystery."

37. Melnyk, "Rudy Wiebe and other rebels," 31. Cf. Wiebe's remark to Heather Robertson: "I've about had it with Western history" (22).

38. Zwarun, 36.

Bibliography

The following bibliography lays no claim to completeness. As religious thinker and, in particular, as first editor of the *Mennonite Brethren Herald,* Rudy Wiebe has written many articles and editorials on Mennonite subjects; these are often of an ephemeral or limited nature, and I have included here only those that throw interesting light on his career and practice as a novelist. A full list of his early writings may be found in Allan Dueck's unpublished M.A. thesis, "Rudy Wiebe as Storyteller: Vision and Art in Wiebe's fiction" (University of Alberta, 1974), pp. 124-29, to which I am much indebted.

The list of secondary materials is similarly selective. I have tried to include all substantial treatments of his work, but, in the case of reviews, I have limited my list to (a) those attaining a standard of literary criticism that renders them of more than passing interest; and (b) those including quotations from interviews with Wiebe.

Wiebe's manuscripts and personal papers are housed in the Library of the University of Calgary. This collection is described briefly in *Canadian Authors, Manuscripts: A Guide to the Collections* (University of Calgary: Occasional Pamphlet no 2, 1978), pp. 12-13.

A.   Books by Wiebe

Peace Shall Destroy Many. Toronto: McClelland and Stewart, 1962; Grand Rapids: Eerdmans, 1964. [Reprinted in the New Canadian Library with an introduction by J.M. Robinson, 1972]

First and Vital Candle. Toronto: McClelland and Stewart; Grand Rapids: Eerdmans, 1966. [Reprinted in paperback by McClelland and Stewart, 1979]

The Blue Mountains of China. Toronto: McClelland and Stewart; Grand Rapids: Eerdmans, 1970. [Reprinted in the New Canadian Library with an introduction by W.J. Keith, 1975]

The Temptations of Big Bear. Toronto: McClelland and Stewart, 1973. [Reprinted in the New Canadian Library with an introduction by Allan Bevan, 1976]

Where Is the Voice Coming From?. Toronto: McClelland and Stewart, 1974. [Short stories]

The Scorched-Wood People. Toronto: McClelland and Stewart, 1977. [Reprinted in the New Canadian Library, 1981]

[In collaboration with Theatre Passe Muraille] *Far As the Eye Can See*. Edmonton: NeWest Press, 1977. [Play]

[With Harry Savage and Tom Radford] *Alberta/A Celebration*. Edmonton: Hurtig, 1979. [Short stories]

The Mad Trapper. Toronto: McClelland and Stewart, 1980.

B.   Books Edited by Wiebe

The Story-Makers. Toronto: Macmillan, 1970.

Stories from Western Canada. Toronto: Macmillan, 1972.

[with Andreas Schroeder] *Stories from Pacific and Arctic Canada*. Toronto: Macmillan, 1974. [Wiebe chose the Arctic selections]

Double Vision: An Anthology of Twentieth-Century Stories in English. Toronto: Macmillan, 1976.

Getting Here: Stories Selected by Rudy Wiebe. Edmonton: NeWest Press, 1970. [No introduction]

[with Aritha van Herk] *More Stories from Western Canada*. Toronto: Macmillan, 1980.

C.   Fiction by Wiebe in Books and Periodicals

"The Midnight Ride of an Alberta Boy," *Liberty*, 33 (September 1956), 22, 64, 66. Revised and reprinted as "Scrapbook" in *WV*.

"The Power," in Earle Birney *et. al.*, eds., *New Voices: Canadian University Writing of 1956* (Toronto: Dent, 1956), pp. 128-33.

"Tudor King," *Christian Living*, 11 (December 1964), 10-11, 31-2. Reprinted in *WV*.

"Incident from a Novel in Progress," *Foolscap* [Goshen College, Indiana], 4 (Spring 1965), 46-53. Incorporated into *FVC*.

"My Life: That's As it Was," *Canadian Mennonite*, 15 (9 instalments, 13 June-15 August 1967). Incorporated into *BMC*.

"Black Vulture," *The Mennonite*, 82 (20 June 1967), 410-15. Reprinted in *Christian Living*, 14 (July 1967), 20-5, and *Mennonite Brethren Herald*, 6 (21 July 1967), 2-6. Incorporated into *BMC*.
[Also translated by Ingrid Janzen as "Der Schwarze Geier," *Der Bote*, 44 (3 instalments, 27 June-11 July 1967)]

"Millstone for the Sun's Day," *Tamarack Review*, no 44 (Summer 1967), 56-64. Reprinted in John Metcalf, ed. *The Narrative Voice* (Toronto: McGraw-Hill Ryerson, 1972), and in *WV*.

"Over the Red Line," *The Mennonite*, 82 (18 July 1967), 464-67. Reprinted in *Christian Living*, 14 (August 1967), 20-3, and *Mennonite Brethren Herald*, 6 (8 September 1967), 4-6. Incorporated into *BMC*.
[Also translated by Ingrid Janzen as "Ueber die rote Linie," *Der Bote*, 44 (2 instalments, 18-25 July 1967)]

"The Well," *The Mennonite*, 82 (15 August 1967), 502-5. Reprinted in *Christian Living*, 14 (September 1967), 20-3, *Mennonite Brethren Herald* 6 (6 October 1967), 4-6, and *Pluck*, 1 (Spring 1968), 31-6. Incorporated into *BMC*.
[Also translated by Ingrid Janzen as "Der Brunnen" in *Der Bote*, 44 (2 instalments, 15-22 August 1967)]

"All on Their Knees," *The Mennonite*, 83 (17 December 1968), 778-83. Reprinted in *Mennonite Brethren Herald*, 10 (3 December 1971), 2-6, and, much revised, in *WV*.

"Did Jesus Ever Laugh?," *Fiddlehead*, no 84 (March-April 1970), 40-52. Reprinted in Rudy Wiebe, ed., *Stories from Western Canada* (Toronto: Macmillan, 1972) and in *WV*.

"The Blue Mountains of China: My Life: That's As It Was," *Mosaic*, III/3 (Spring 1970), 154-61. Incorporated into *BMC*.

"Oolulik," in *The Story-Makers* (Toronto: Macmillan, 1970), pp. 275-92. Originally a chapter in *FVC*, here first published (by Wiebe himself) as a short story.

"Where is the Voice Coming From?," in David Helwig and Tom Marshall, eds., *Fourteen Stories High* (Ottawa: Oberon, 1971), pp. 112-21. Reprinted in John Metcalf, ed., *The Narrative Voice* (Toronto: McGraw-Hill Ryerson, 1970) and in *WV*.

"Bluecoats on the Sacred Hill of the Wild Peas," in John H. Redekop, ed., *The Star-Spangled Beaver* (Toronto: Peter Martin Associates, 1971), pp. 46-54. Reprinted in *WV*.

"The Fish Caught in the Battle River," *White Pelican*, 1 (Fall 1971), 33-7. Reprinted in *WV*.

"The Grand Pursuit of Big Bear," *Fiddlehead*, no 95 (Fall 1972), 3-12. Incorporated into *TBB*.

"Along the Red Deer and the South Saskatchewan," *Prism (International)*, 12 (Spring 1973), 47-56. Reprinted in *WV*.

"Buffalo Run," *Journal of Canadian Fiction*, 2 (Spring 1973), 39-41. Incorporated into *TBB*.

"How the People Used to Make Treaties," *White Pelican*, 3 (Spring 1973), 58-64. Incorporated into *TBB*.

"The Naming of Albert Johnson," *Queen's Quarterly*, 80 (Autumn 1973), 370-78. Reprinted in Andreas Schroeder and Rudy Wiebe, eds., *Stories from Pacific and Arctic Canada* (Toronto: Macmillan, 1974) and in *WV*.

"Games for Queen Victoria," *Saturday Night*, 91 (March 1976), 61-7. Reprinted in Rudy Wiebe and Aritha van Herk, eds., *More Stories from Western Canada*. (Toronto: Macmillan, 1980).

"Home for Night," *NeWest Review*, 1 (April 1976), 6-7, 9.

"Hunting McDougall," *Fiddlehead*, no 108 (Winter 1976), 17-24. Incorporated into *SWP*.

"Batoche. May 12, 1885." in Gary Geddes, ed., *Divided We Stand* (Toronto: Peter Martin Associates, 1977), pp. 26-30. Incorporated into *SWP*.

"The Year We Gave Away the Land," *Week-End Magazine* (Toronto *Globe and Mail*), 9 July 1977, 14. Reprinted in *AC*.

"In the Beaver Hills," in Morris Wolfe, ed., *Aurora: New Canadian Writing 1978* (Toronto: Doubleday Canada, 1978), 71-80.

"After Thirty Years of Marriage," *Canadian Forum*, 58 (October-November 1978), 36-40. Reprinted in *AC*.

"Chinook Christmas," *NeWest Review*, 4 (December 1978), 8-9, 12. Reprinted in *AC*.

"The Good Maker," *Mennonite Brethren Herald*, 18 (16 February 1979), 7-10.

"An Indication of Burning," *Canadian Fiction Magazine*, no 32/3 (1979-80), 150-64.

D.   Articles and Reviews by Wiebe

"An Author Speaks About His Novel," *Canadian Mennonite*, 11 (11 April 1963), 8. [On *PDM*] Reprinted in *VL*.

"For the Mennonite Churches: A Last Chance," *Christian Living*, 11 (June 1964), 26-8. Reprinted in *VL*.

"Tombstone Community," *Mennonite Life*, 19 (October 1964), 150-53. Reprinted in *VL*.

"The Artist as a Critic and a Witness," *Christian Living*, 12 (March 1965), 20-3, 40. Reprinted (as "The Artist as Witness to and Critic of Society") in *Journal of Church and Society*, 1 (Fall 1965), 45-57, and in *VL*.

"Moros and Mennonites in the Chaco of Paraguay," *Canadian Mennonite*, 14 (29 November 1966), 1, 7. Reprinted in *VL*.

"The Peter Neudorfs of Filadelfia, Paraguay," *Christian Living*, 14 (May 1967), 4-6.

"The Meaning of Being Mennonite Brethren," *Mennonite Brethren Herald*, 9 (17 April 1970), 2-4. Reprinted in *VL*.

"Passage by Land," *Canadian Literature*, no 48 (Spring 1971), 25-7. Reprinted with an additional section in John Metcalf, ed., *The Narrative Voice* (Toronto: McGraw-Hill Ryerson, 1972), pp. 257-60.

"Pushed Back to the Ridge," *Canadian Literature*, no 48 (Spring 1971), 86-7. [Review of Mort Forer, *The Humback*]

"Western Canadian Fiction: Past and Future," *Western American Literature*, 6 (Spring 1971), 21-31.

"A Clutch of Books About Indians," *White Pelican*, 1 (Fall 1971), 61-3. [Review of Marty Dunn, *Red or White;* Sarain Stump, *There Is My People Sleeping;* James Stephens, *Sacred Legends of the Sandy Lake Cree;* Alexander Morris, *The Treaties of Canada with the Indians of Manitoba and the North-West Territories* (reprint)]

"Guys Who Stay Out in the Cold," *Books in Canada*, 1 (December 1971), 7-8. [Review of Fred Bruemmer, *Seasons of the Eskimo* and Duncan Pryde, *Nunaga: My Land, My Country*]

"Songs of the Canadian Eskimo," *Canadian Literature*, no 52 (Spring 1972), 57-69.

"A Literary Mismatch," *Books in Canada*, 2 (January-February 1973), 30-1. [Review of Fraser Sutherland, *The Style of Innocence*]

"More storytellers are needed," *Mennonite Reporter*, 3 (19 February 1973), 10.

"Wise and witty testaments," *Edmonton Journal* (3 November 1973). [Review of Edward Ahenakew, *Voices of the Plains Cree*]

"On the Trail of Big Bear," *Journal of Canadian Fiction*, 3, no 2 (1974), 45-8. Reprinted in *VL*.

"The Year of the Indian," *Dalhousie Review*, 54 (Spring 1974), 164-67. [Review of C. Frank Turner, *Across the Medicine Line;* Lovat Dickson, *Wilderness Man;* Robert Kroetsch, *Gone Indian*]

"All That's Left of Big Bear," *Maclean's*, 88 (September 1975), 53-5. Reprinted in its original, longer form in *VL*, under the original title, "Bear Spirit in a Strange Land."

"Riel: A Possible Film Treatment," *NeWest Review*, 1 (June 1975), 6. Reprinted in *VL*.

"In the west, Sir John A. is a bastard and Riel a saint. Ever ask why?," *Toronto Globe and Mail* (25 March 1978). Reprinted in *VL*.

"A Novelists's Personal Notes on Frederick Philip Grove," *University of Toronto Quarterly*, 47 (Spring 1978), 189-99. Reprinted in *VL*.

"The Death and Life of Albert Johnson: Collected Notes on a Possible Legend," in Diane Bessai and David Jackel, eds., *Figures in a Ground: Canadian Essays on Modern Literature Collected in Honor of Sheila Watson* (Saskatoon: Western Producer Prairie Books, 1978), pp. 219-46.

"New Land, Ancient Land," in Richard Chadbourne and Hallvard Dahlie, eds., *The New Land: Studies in a Literary Theme* (Waterloo: Wilfrid Laurier University Press [for the Calgary Institute for the Humanities], 1978), 1-4.

Untitled Review of Edith Fowke, *Folklore of Canada, University of Toronto; Quarterly*, 47 (Summer 1978), 476-77.

E.   Criticism

Adachi, Ken. "Unusual author lives a life of Canadian example," *Toronto Star* (4 November 1977). [Quotes briefly from interview with Wiebe]

———. "Wiebe attacks Arctic trapper movie," *Toronto Sunday Star* (21 September 1980). [Quotes from interview with Wiebe]

Barbour, Douglas. "Big Bear speak with awesome tongue," *Edmonton Journal* (21 September 1973). [Review of *TBB*]

——— *"The Scorched-Wood People,"* *Pacific Northwest Review of Books* (May 1978), 14. [Review of *SWP*]

Bergman, Brian. "Rudy Wiebe: Story-Maker of the Prairies," *Gateway* [University of Alberta] (10 November 1977), 9, 11. [Interview] Reprinted in *VL*.

Bilan, R.P. "Wiebe and Religious Struggle," *Canadian Literature, no 77* (Summer 1978), 50-63. [On *BMC*]

——— "Fiction" [annual column], *University of Toronto Quarterly*, 47 (Summer 1978), 335-38. [Review of *SWP*] Reprinted in *VL*.

Cameron, Donald. "Rudy Wiebe: The Moving Stream is Perfectly at Rest," in his *Conversations with Canadian Novelists, Part Two* (Toronto: Macmillan 1973), pp. 146-60. [Interview]

Carpenter, Dave. Untitled review of *TBB, University of Manitoba Alumni Journal* (Fall 1973). [Quotes briefly from interview with Wiebe]

Chatelin, Ray. "Tragic Story of Big Bear," *Vancouver Province* (4 December 1973). [Review of *TBB*, including quotations from interview with Wiebe]

Cohen, Joy-Ann. "Author Rudy Wiebe trying movies as a way to 'reach' mass audience," *Calgary Herald* (14 October 1978). [Quotes from interview with Wiebe]

Dawe, Alan. "Untaped Interviews," *Event*, 4 (1974), 33-40. [Includes interview with Wiebe]

De Vos, Karen R. "Of Peace and Violence: A Discussion of Rudy Wiebe's Novels," *The Banner* [official organ of Christian Reformed Church] (9 April 1971), 16-17.

Doerksen, D.W. "Looking for a Place to Call Their Own," *Mennonite Brethren Herald* (22 January 1971), 22-3. [Review of *BMC*]

Doerksen, Victor G. "The Style of *Peace Shall Destroy Many*," *Aion, a Journal of Cogitation* [Winnipeg], 3 (May 1963), 13-15.

Dueck, Allan. "A Sense of the Past," *Journal of Canadian Fiction*, 2 (Fall 1973), 88-91. [Review of *TBB*]

——— "Rudy Wiebe as Storyteller: Vision and Art in Wiebe's Fiction." Unpublished M.A. thesis: University of Alberta, 1974.

——— "Rudy Wiebe's Approach to Historical Fiction: A Study of *The Temptations of Big Bear* and *The Scorched-Wood People*," in John Moss, ed., *The Canadian Novel: Here and Now* (Toronto: NC Press, 1978), pp. 182-200.

Duerksen, David. "Theological Straw or Immemorial Stone?," *Aion, a Journal of Cogitation* [Winnipeg], 3 (May 1963), 16-23. [On *PDM*]

Erb, Marsha. "An author's view of his homeland," *Saskatoon Star-Phoenix* (2 November 1973). [Quotes from interview with Wiebe]

Ferris, Ina. "Religious Vision and Fictional Form: Rudy Wiebe's *The Blue Mountains of China*," *Mosaic*, XI/3 (Spring 1978), 79-85. Reprinted in *VL*.

Friesen, James. "Fiction and the Tradition of Truth," *Aion, a Journal of Cogitation* [Winnipeg], 3 (May 1963), 5-12. [On *PDM*]

Giesbrecht, Herbert. " 'O Life, How Naked and How Hard When Known!' A Comprehensive Review of a Controversial Novel That Destroyed the Peace of Many," *Canadian Mennonite*, 11 (22 March 1963), 5, 8-9. [Review of *PDM*] Reprinted in *VL*.

Hancock, Maxine. "Wiebe: A Voice Crying in the Wilderness," *Christianity Today*, 23 (16 February 1979), 30-1.

Harlton, Howard. "He's doing novel justice to the Indians," *Edmonton Journal* (21 September 1973). [On *TBB*; quotes from interview with Wiebe]

Jacub, George. "Louis Riel visionary, not madman: Wiebe," *Winnipeg Tribune* (4 November 1977). [Review of *SWP* combined with interview]

Jeffrey, David L. "Biblical Hermeneutic and Family History in Contemporary Canadian Fiction: Wiebe and Laurence," *Mosaic*, XI/3 (Spring 1978), 87-106. [On *BMC*]

——— "A Search for Peace: Prophecy and Parable in the Fiction of Rudy Wiebe," in W.J. Keith, ed., *A Voice in the Land: Essays By and About Rudy Wiebe* (Edmonton: NeWest Press, 1981), pp. 179-201.

Keith, W.J. "From Document to Art: Wiebe's Historical Short Stories and Their Sources," *Studies in Canadian Literature*, 4 (Summer 1979), 106-19.

——— ed. *A Voice in the Land: Essays By and About Rudy Wiebe*. Edmonton: NeWest Press, 1981.

Klassen, Peter. "Peace! And There Is No Peace," *Mennonite Brethren Herald* (12 October 1962). [Review of *PDM*]

Kroetsch, Robert. "Unhiding the Hidden: Recent Canadian Fiction," *Journal of Canadian Fiction*, 3, no 3 (1974), 43-5. [On *TBB*]

Mandel, Eli. "Where the Voice Comes From," *Quill and Quire*, 40 (December 1974), 4, 20. [Interview] Reprinted in *VL*.

Mansbridge, Francis. "Wiebe's Sense of Community," *Canadian Literature*, no 77 (Summer 1978), 42-9. [On *PDM*]

Martinson, F.G. "Meet Rudy Wiebe," *Canadian Review*, 1 (April 1974), 9. [Interview]

Melnyk, George. "The Western Canadian Imagination: An Interview with Rudy Wiebe," *Canadian Fiction Magazine*, no 12 (Winter 1974), 29-34. [Interview] Reprinted in *VL*.

——— "Rudy Wiebe and other rebels," *Quill and Quire*, 43 (November 1977), 31. [Review of *SWP* combined with interview]

"Mennonite author will stay in West," *Kitchener-Waterloo Record* (22 July 1974). [Quotes from interview with Wiebe]

Morley, Patricia A. *The Comedians: Hugh Hood and Rudy Wiebe*. Toronto: Clarke Irwin, 1977.

Moss, John. "Genocide: The White Man's Burden," in his *Sex and Violence in the Canadian Novel: The Ancestral Present* (Toronto: McClelland and Stewart, 1977), pp. 256-73. [On *TBB*]

Neuman, Shirley. "Unearthing Language: An Interview with Rudy Wiebe and Robert Kroetsch," in W.J. Keith, ed., *A Voice in the Land: Essays By and About Rudy Wiebe* (Edmonton: NeWest Press, 1981), pp. 226-47. [Interview]

"New book champions unsung Indian hero," *Winnipeg Tribune* (19 October 1973). [Unsigned review of *TBB* including quotations from interview with Wiebe]

Nickel, James W. "A Conversation with Rudy Wiebe," *The Sceptic* [Tabor College, Hillsboro, Kansas], 1 (Spring 1964), 24-30. [Interview]

Peetoom, Adrian. "The Effects of Rudy Wiebe," *Vanguard* [Christian Action Foundation, Woodbridge, Ontario], 1 (August-September 1972), 4-5. [On *PDM, FVC, BMC*]

Pomer, B. Untitled review of *FVC, Canadian Forum*, 47 (January 1968), 235-36.

Redekop, Magdalene. "Translated into the Past: Language in *The Blue Mountains of China*," in W.J. Keith, ed., *A Voice in the Land: Essays By and About Rudy Wiebe* (Edmonton: NeWest Press, 1981), pp. 97-123.

——— *Rudy Wiebe*. Profiles in Canadian Literature. Toronto: Dundurn Press, 1981. [Pamphlet]

Reimer, E.E. "Rudy Wiebe's 'Steel Lines of Fiction': The Progress of a Mennonite Novelist," *Mennonite Mirror*, 1 (September 1971), 7, 27-9.

Reimer, Margaret and Sue Steiner, "Translating life into art: A conversation with Rudy Wiebe," *Mennonite Reporter*, 3 (26 November 1973), section A, 7-8. [Interview] Reprinted in *VL*.

Rickard, D'Arcy. "Rudy Wiebe to study Paraguay Mennonites," *Lethbridge Herald* (11 July 1968). [Quotes from interview with Wiebe]

Robertson, Heather. "Western Mystic," *Canadian Magazine* [*Toronto Star*] (10 December 1977), 20, 22. [Quotes from interview with Wiebe]

"Rudy Wiebe, Novelist; Vindicator and Christian," *Festival Quarterly* [Lancaster, Pennsylvania] (August-October 1978), 17, 31. [Quotes from interview with Wiebe]

Saunders, Tom. "The Causerie," *Winnipeg Free Press* (20 April 1963). [Review of *PDM*]

——— "The Causerie," *Winnipeg Free Press* (18 June 1966). [Quotes briefly from interview with Wiebe]

——— "Growing Pains—and Growth," *Winnipeg Free Press* (9 July 1966). [Review of *FVC*]

Scobie, Stephen. "For Goodness' Sake," *Books in Canada*, 9 (February 1980), 3-5. [Quotes from interview with Wiebe]

Sheppard, June. "Nothing quaint about him," *Edmonton Journal* (3 December 1970). [Quotes from interview with Wiebe]

Solecki, Sam. Untitled review of *SWP, Fiddlehead*, no 177 (Spring 1978), 117-20. Reprinted in *VL*.

——— "Giant Fictions and Large Meanings: The Novels of Rudy Wiebe," *Canadian Forum*, 60 (March 1981), 5-8, 13.

Stephens, Donald. "A World Sequestered," *Canadian Literature*, no 63 (Winter 1975), 102-3. [Review of *WV*]

Struthers, J.R. (Tim). "Reader engaged in dialogue with darkness," *London Free Press* (1 February 1975). [Review of *WV*]

Suderman, Elmer F. "Universal Values in *Peace Shall Destroy Many*," *Mennonite Life*, 20 (October 1965), 172-76. Reprinted in *VL*.

Taylor, Lauralyn. *"The Temptations of Big Bear:* A Filmic Novel?," *Essays on Canadian Writing*, 9 (Winter 1977-78), 134-38.

Tefs, Wayne A. "Where is Your Voice Coming From, Rudy Wiebe?," *Canadian Dimension*, 13, no 2 (1978), 51-2.

——— "Rudy Wiebe: Mystery and Reality," *Mosaic*, XI/4 (Summer 1978), 155-58.

Tiessen, Hildegaard E. "A Mighty Inner River: Peace in the Fiction of Rudy Wiebe," *Journal of Canadian Fiction*, 2 (Fall 1973), 71-6. Reprinted in revised form in John Moss, ed., *The Canadian Novel: Here and Now* (Toronto: NC Press, 1978), pp. 169-81.

Twigg, Alan. "Of Moral Fiction," *NeWest Review*, 5 (January 1980), 4-5, 12. [Interview] Reprinted as "Public Eye" in his *For Openers: Conversations with 24 Canadian Writers* (Madiera Park, B.C.: Harbour Publishing, 1981), pp. 207-18.

Williams, David. "The Indian Our Ancestor: Three Modes of Vision in Recent Canadian Fiction," *Dalhousie Review*, 58 (Summer 1978), 309-28.

Woodcock, George. "Riel & Dumont," *Canadian Literature*, no 77 (Summer 1978), 98-100. [Review of *SWP*]

Zilm, Glennis. Syndicated review of *BMC*, appearing under varying titles in numerous local newspapers including *Medicine Hat News* (17 April 1971), *St. Catharines Standard* (27 February 1971), and *Peterborough Examiner* (8 March 1971). [Quotes briefly from interview with Wiebe]

Zwarun, Suzanne. "Lonely are the grave," *Maclean's*, 91 (4 September 1978), 34-7. [Quotes from interview with Wiebe]

F.   Background Studies, etc. (A Selective List)

Allen, R.S. "Big Bear," *Saskatchewan History*, 25 (1972), 1-17.

Bowsfield, H[artwell], ed. *Louis Riel: Rebel of the Western Frontier or Victim of Politics and Prejudice?* Toronto: Copp Clark, 1969.

Brodie, Neil. *Twelve Days with the Indians, May 14-May 26, 1885: Being his Experiences in Poundmaker's Camp During the Rebellion of 1885.* Battleford: Saskatchewan Herald, 1932. [Pamphlet]

Coulter, John. *Riel.* Toronto: Ryerson, 1962. [Play]

——— *The Trial of Louis Riel.* Ottawa: Oberon, 1968. [Play]

De Fehr, William *et al.*, eds. *Harvest: Anthology of Mennonite Writing in Canada.* Centennial Committee of the Mennonite Historical Society of Manitoba, 1974.

Dyck, Cornelius, ed. *An Introduction to Mennonite History: A popular history of the Anabaptists and the Mennonites.* Scottdale, Pennsylvania: Herald Press, 1967.

Dyck, Harvey L. "Collectivization, Depression, and Immigration, 1929-1930: A Chance Interplay," in Harvey L. Dyck and H. Peter Krosby, eds., *Empire and Nations: Essays in Honour of Frederic H. Soward.* Toronto: University of Toronto Press in association with the University of British Columbia, 1969, pp. 144-59.

Epp, Frank H. *Mennonite Exodus.* Altona, Manitoba: D.W. Friesen, 1962.

Flanagan, Thomas. *Louis 'David' Riel: Prophet of the New World.* Toronto: University of Toronto Press, 1979.

——— ed. *The Diaries of Louis Riel.* Edmonton: Hurtig, 1976.

Francis, E.K. *In Search of Utopia: The Mennonites in Manitoba.* Altona, Manitoba: D.W. Friesen, 1955.

Fraser, William B. *Big Bear, Indian Patriot.* Calgary: Historical Society of Alberta, 1966. [Pamphlet]

Gutteridge, Don. *Riel: A Poem for Voices.* [1968] Toronto: Van Nostrand Reinhold, 1972.

Harrison, Dick. *Unnamed Country: The Struggle for a Canadian Prairie Fiction.* Edmonton: University of Alberta Press, 1977.

Howard, Joseph Kinsey. *Strange Empire: A Narrative of the Northwest.* Introduction by Bernard de Voto. New York: Morrow, 1952. Reprinted in paperback under the title *Strange Empire: Louis Riel and the Métis People* with a new introduction by Martin Robin. Toronto: James Lewis and Samuel, 1974.

Hughes, Stuart, ed. *The Frog Lake 'Massacre': Personal Perspectives on Ethnic Conflict.* Toronto: McClelland and Stewart, 1976. [Contains a version of William Bleasdell Cameron's memoir, *The War Trail of Big Bear*, reprints *Two Months in the Camp of Big Bear: The Life and Adventures of Theresa Gowanlock and Theresa Delaney*, etc.]

Jenness, Diamond. *The Indians of Canada* [1932]. Seventh ed. Toronto: University of Toronto Press, 1977.

Lohrenz, Gerhard. *The Mennonites of Western Canada.* Steinbach, Manitoba: Derksen Printers, 1974. [Pamphlet]

Lukács, Georg. *The Historical Novel.* Translated from the German by Hannah and Stanley Mitchell [1962]. Harmondsworth: Penguin Books, 1969.

Morton, Desmond. *The Last War Drum.* Toronto: Hakkert, 1972.

——— ed. *The Queen v. Louis Riel.* Toronto: University of Toronto Press, 1974.

North, Dick. *The Mad Trapper of Rat River.* Toronto: Macmillan, 1972.

Pryde, Duncan. *Nunaga: My Land, My Country.* Edmonton: Hurtig, 1971.

Stanley, George F.G. *The Birth of Western Canada* [1936]. Toronto: University of Toronto Press, 1960.

——— *Louis Riel.* Toronto: Ryerson Press, 1963.

Stegner, Wallace. *Wolf Willow: A History, a Story, and a Memoir of the Last Plains Frontier* [1955]. New York: Viking, 1968.

Suderman, Elmer F. "Fiction and Mennonite Life," *Midcontinent American Studies Journal*, 10 (Spring 1969), 16-24.

Thiessen, J. "Canadian Mennonite Literature," *Canadian Literature*, no 52 (Winter 1972), 65-72.

Woodcock, George. *Gabriel Dumont: The Métis Chief and his Lost World*. Edmonton: Hurtig, 1975.

Yoder, John Howard. *The Politics of Jesus*. Grand Rapids, Michigan: Eerdmans, 1972.

Index

WOMEN OF SPORTS

THE BEST OF THE BEST
in
Track & Field

BY
RACHEL RUTLEDGE

M

THE MILLBROOK PRESS
BROOKFIELD, CONNECTICUT

Produced by
CRONOPIO PUBLISHING
John Sammis, President
and
TEAM STEWART, INC.

Series Design and Electronic Page Makeup by
JAFFE ENTERPRISES
Ron Jaffe

Researched and Edited by
Mark Stewart, Michael Kennedy, and Mariah Morgan

All photos courtesy AP/WIDE WORLD PHOTOS, INC.
except the following:
TEAM STEWART — Page 12
TONY DUFFY/THE SPORTING IMAGE — Page 16, 26, 37, 52
VICTAH SAILER/PHOTO RUN — Page 14, 28, 31, 34, 56, 61
JACK MCMANUS/PHOTO RUN — Page 55, 58
DAN HELMS — Page 40

Published by
The Millbrook Press, Inc.
2 Old New Milford Road
Brookfield, Connecticut   06804

Library of Congress Cataloging-in-Publication Data

Rutledge, Rachel.
  Women of Sports. The best of the best in track & field / by Rachel Rutledge.
      p.   cm.
  Includes index.
  Summary: Discusses the past and present of women's track and field and presents
biographies of eight notable competitors, including Sally Barsosio, Cathy Freeman, and
Angela Williams.
  ISBN 0-7613-1300-1 (lib. bdg.).—ISBN 0-7613-0446-0 (pbk.)
  1. Track and field athletes—Biography—Juvenile literature.   2. Women track and field
athletes—Biography—Juvenile literature.   3. Track–athletics for women—Juvenile literature.
[1. Track and field athletes. 2. Women—Biography.] I. Title.   II. Title: Best of the best in
track & field.
GV697.A1R89 1999
796.42'092'2—dc21
                                                                                                    98-51645
                                                                                                         CIP
                                                                                                         AC

pbk: 10 9 8 7 6 5 4 3 2 1
lib: 10 9 8 7 6 5 4 3 2 1